Minidrill

Fifteen Projects

Minidrill

Fifteen Projects

John Everett

Guild of Master Craftsman Publications Ltd

First published 1999 by
Guild of Master Craftsman Publications Ltd,
166 High Street, Lewes,
East Sussex, BN7 1XU

ISBN 1 86108 137 5

Finished item photographs by Anthony Bailey
Step-by-step photographs and line drawings by John Everett

Designed by Paul Griffin
Cover design by Wheelhouse Design
Typeface: Stone Serif
Colour origination by Viscan Graphics (Singapore)
Printed in Great Britain at the University Press, Cambridge

CONTENTS

Introduction

If you already have a minidrill or are contemplating buying one and want to be able to use it for more than just drilling holes, this is the book for you.

The minidrill, with its attachments and accessories, has become universally available and, once it is mastered, can provide hours of worthwhile enjoyment for the user whether you are involved in crafts, modelling, miniature engineering or any other type of project.

In most respects, the minidrill is identical to its larger counterpart. It is basically a small-scale drill which can accept a variety of accessories and 'add-ons', making it adaptable to virtually any purpose. The minidrill's main advantage is that it can work on very small projects, ones which would prove far too intricate for a full-size drill.

Several companies make minidrills, with more coming on to the market all the time. The range of accessories is also increasing rapidly. This is good news for the hobbyist and craft worker. Several of the major accessories are too costly for most budgets. The first four projects in this book explain how to make some of these items, enabling you to put together your own at a fraction of the cost of the ready-made accessories.

At first glance, the minidrill and the basic kit might seem insignificant. Don't be misled by this initial impression as the minidrill with its accessories is a serious tool capable of a huge variety of different tasks and projects. More and more can be accomplished with this versatile equipment, particularly as new accessories and add-ons for the minidrill are coming onto the market all the time.

This book will outline the many techniques which are applicable to the minidrill. Each technique is illustrated through a project you can make, so that you will gain the necessary practical experience to become fully competent in the use of the minidrill and its many accessories. The projects are intended to familiarize you with the possibilities of the tool, and to build your confidence so that you can think up new ideas for yourself in the future.

All of the minidrill equipment used throughout this book is made by the firm Minicraft, but there are many other brands of minidrill equipment available, all of which will come with suitable accessories and add-ons for these projects.

The projects featured in this book rely on the basic minidrill, or the engraving tool, with the various accessories, although a few extra tools will be needed occasionally. The materials needed are reasonably cheap and are easily obtained through most good DIY and craft outlets.

CHAPTER 1

The basics

Most minidrill owners will already have the basic hobby drill kit. This kit usually consists of the basic drill, a power unit to enable the drill to use mains electricity directly and an assortment of accessories which can be used with the drill.

SOME USEFUL TIPS

While the motors in these drills are becoming more powerful they can never have the degree of power or torque of a modest full-size drill. They are suited to dealing with small-scale projects, but they are not designed for rough treatment. Never try to force a drill to work harder than it should. If you need to push to achieve the effect you want, then the chances are that your drill bit is blunt. Sharpen it, or change it for another, but don't try to force the drill to cut faster than it is capable of doing.

Remember that the minidrill is a precision tool and it must be treated as such. Most minidrill accessories, such as bits and burrs, are not that expensive to buy or replace as they become worn out. A little care taken when using them will considerably prolong their

► The basic minidrill with power adaptor

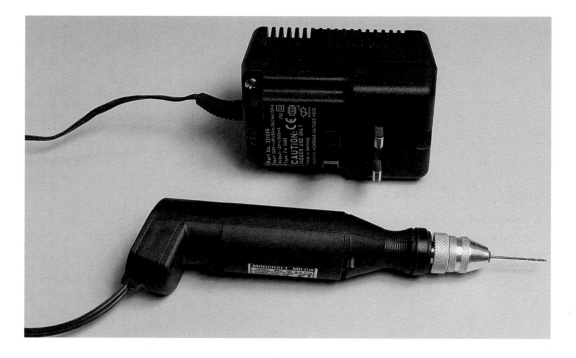

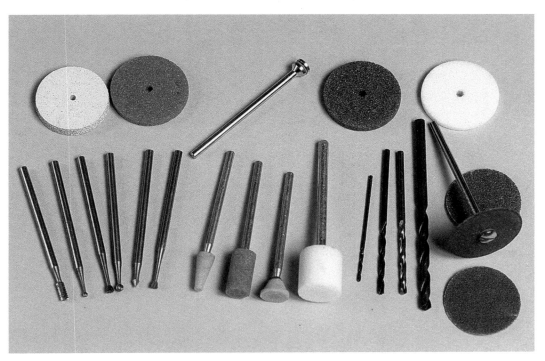

◄ An assortment of burrs, grinders, sanding discs and drill bits usually supplied with the standard hobby kit

working lives. Grinding wheels can suffer from being used under too much pressure, so treat them gently and always let the tool do the work, rather than adding extra pressure yourself. You will find that the smaller drill bits are difficult to sharpen effectively without a magnifying glass. This is true also of the smaller burrs.

DRILL SPEED

The main characteristic of the basic minidrill is its speed of rotation. This speed tends to be very much faster than its bigger counterpart. A high speed of rotation can lead to problems when using some materials, such as plastics, because the friction generated tends to make the material distort and sometimes even burn. On the other hand, the high drill speed makes precision cutting and carving much easier and more effective.

It is highly desirable to have some kind of drill speed control for the projects which follow. Drills at the top end of the market have a speed control facility built into their power units. Many standard drills do not have a variable speed control supplied as standard, but have a suitable adapter unit available as an optional extra. It is also worth checking with your local electronics store, who can usually be relied on to come up with a suitable alternative for lowering the speed of the motor in your drill.

MINIDRILL ACCESSORIES

The accessories will normally include two or three small drill bits, a mandrel, a couple of different cutting wheels and a grinding wheel. There will also be several burrs of different shapes. These are essentially rotary files or cutters and can be used to form and shape a variety of materials. Some kits will also include a sanding backing pad and small round sanding discs for use with the mandrel. Refer to the maker of your minidrill's catalogue to discover what accessories are available, and what the working parameter of each tool is.

DRILL BITS

The drill bits supplied by most, if not all, manufacturers of minidrills and their accessories will be of the high-speed twist type. These bits will be suitable for use on mild steel and non-ferrous metals, like brass and copper, as well as wood and plastics. Generally speaking, specialist drill bits, such as those for wood and masonry, are not of a suitable size for the minidrill (up to around 2.5mm/³⁄₃₂in). A normal high-speed twist drill will work effectively on most materials.

MANDREL

This is a simple stick-like device with a screw fitting situated in one end and the other end fixes into the chuck of the minidrill, allowing the user to mount a number of useful accessories including grinding and cutting wheels. All these items will have a hole in their centre so that they can be mounted on the mandrel. Remove the screw in the mandrel, pass it through the centre of the accessory, replace the screw in the mandrel and simply tighten it with a screwdriver. Then, you can simply fix the complete tool into the drill chuck and use it securely and easily for a variety of purposes.

GRINDING WHEELS

Flat grinding wheels are often supplied with the basic minidrill kit. They come in a variety of grit sizes and are often colour coded for easy identification: brown for fine grit, white for medium grit and pink for coarse grit.

The main use of this tool is for grinding ceramics, metals, stones and glass. It can also be used to sharpen and de-rust metal items.

Most minidrill kits also include grinding wheels which have their own spindle for inserting directly into the minidrill chuck.

CUTTING WHEELS

These are used with a mandrel (as outlined earlier) and can cut steel and other hard materials, such as model railway rails and the metal frames of model boats and aircraft. They are also used for precision cutting of metal tubes – brass, copper and steel, for instance. They are also ideal for cutting new slots in old worn screws to make them easier to remove.

BURRS

These little rotary files and cutters come into their own when carving wood and soft metals. They are often supplied in a kit in a variety of shapes and sizes to cater for a wide range of cutting and carving applications. It is worth trying each type on a piece of scrap material before using them on a project. You will need to become accustomed to the cutting action of each burr, and determine the most effective drill speed for the tool.

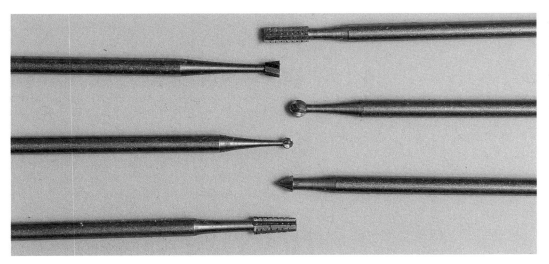

◄ The variety of different burr shapes available enables a large range of cutting tasks to be tackled

You can also buy sets of diamond-coated burrs which are excellent rotary files for precision grinding, shaping and smoothing on any material, no matter how hard. These burrs work best, and will last longest, if used at the drill's maximum speed.

SANDING DISCS

These are supplied in coarse, medium and fine grades and are used with the rubber pad supplied with many kits. The discs can sand easily in awkward spaces and are capable of removing large amounts of material in a very short space of time due to the high rotation speed of the minidrill.

ENGRAVING TOOLS

Engraving can be undertaken with a purpose-made kit or with a minidrill fitted with the appropriate accessories.

An engraving pen is available from the several manufacturers of minidrill equipment, and is intended specifically for engraving on glass and metals. The tool consists of a miniature motorized

pen which rotates the engraving point at high speed, making it easy to follow a complex pattern. The basic engraving kit comes with an engraving point for fine work, and a couple of grinding wheels for removing larger areas with an engraved design.

The engraving pen will not take the usual range of minidrill accessories, but the minidrill can also be used for engraving with equal success. A range of engraving points, including diamond-coated types, is available for use with the standard minidrill.

▼ An engraving pen fitted with a standard engraving bit, along with two shaped grinders

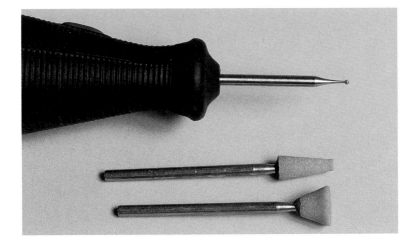

CHAPTER 2

Materials

If you are new to minidrill work, it is a good idea to get hold of small pieces of different types of material such as hardwood, softwood, man-made sheet material like MDF or ply, brass, glass and acrylic sheet, to simply try out the various tools in your minidrill. Try cutting and shaping in order to see just how each burr or drill bit works with different materials. You will then be able to see how the minidrill copes with different types of material and compare how each performs under various conditions.

The advantage of working small is that much, if not all, of the material you need for the projects can be obtained cheaply or for free as offcuts from full-size projects. It pays to shop around; perhaps there is a friendly local woodworker who could provide little pieces of different types of wood.

MAN-MADE MATERIALS
MDF (medium density fibreboard) is used in some of the projects. This can produce a lot of 'micro-dust' when it is being worked. The individual particles of dust are much smaller than usual and can be an irritant, particularly if you happen to be predisposed to respiratory tract problems such as asthma. Always wear a dust mask when working this

material and if you have a dust extraction facility have it in use. A thorough clean-up with a vacuum cleaner after working MDF is a good idea, to avoid an accumulation of dust.

Acrylics and similar materials need to be cut at a lower speed. If you cannot change the speed of your drill, use very light cuts, each of a short duration to avoid heat build-up in the material. Allow a short interval for the material to cool down between each application of the drill.

NATURAL MATERIALS
The high rotation speed of the minidrill can be a positive advantage with many materials. It is perfect for miniature routing operations, producing a smooth finish on many softwoods which would otherwise tend to 'feather'.

Several of the projects outlined in this book use scraps of hardwood and the minidrill is an ideal tool for producing small precisely cut parts.

Too much pressure on the tool can lead to chars and burns, even on many hardwoods. To repair the damage caused by charring it will usually be necessary to cut away the damaged parts of the material, leading to inaccuracies in the finished project. It is better to start with a very light cut and increase pressure

GLASS

When working glass with an engraving tool, it is a good idea to wear protective goggles in case small chips break off during cutting. This is unlikely to happen, however, unless you are applying too much pressure on to the engraving point.

Give the glass a good clean before you begin engraving, as smears on the glass can distort the pattern being copied and make the engraving point slip, causing inaccuracies. Almost any cleaner can be used to give the glass a quick clean, from window cleaner to washing-up liquid. Finish off with a soft, clean cloth.

▲ A selection of hardwoods and softwoods, man-made boards and acrylic

Safety

There is nothing that is inherently dangerous about using a mini-drill, providing some common-sense precautions are observed. Bear in mind that a minidrill, in spite of its size, is an item of high-speed rotating machinery. As such, it needs to be treated with respect. There are unlikely to be any life-threatening situations caused by the minidrill but some inconvenient and uncomfortable minor injuries could well be inflicted upon the unwary.

Be careful with loose clothing and long hair which could become caught in the rapidly rotating chuck. Wearing a normal workshop overall and pinning your hair back will solve this potential problem. When you consider that the chuck of a mini-drill rotates at well over 20,000 revolutions per minute, you will realize that it will take only a small fraction of a second for a loose strand of hair to wrap itself around whatever tool is in use and then the operator will receive a tear-jerking wrench to his or her hair.

It is important to wear a dust mask and safety goggles when appropriate, for example when working with materials like MDF or glass.

Check on a regular basis that the drill cables are in good condition. Many drills operate on low voltage, but increasingly there are mains-operated models available which do not operate on low voltage. A damaged cable can create a potentially dangerous situation. If you operate a mains-operated type of minidrill, use a residual current circuit breaker (RCCB).

Finally, remember that the little drill bits and burrs are very sharp cutting tools. Bearing that in mind, it will be obvious they could cause a nasty cut to the hand or the finger, in spite of their small size. Take the proper precautions, and be sensible when using the drill and you should be fine.

▼ An effective dust mask is a worthwhile investment

METRIC/IMPERIAL CONVERSION

It is time consuming and sometimes difficult to convert accurately between metric and imperial measurements. This is particularly true when it comes to the range of tiny drill bits used with the minidrill. This conversion chart shows fractions of inches with a metric scale alongside for instant comparison.

Using the chart is very simple. For example, if you require a hole 4mm in diameter, find 4mm on the metric part of the chart and then simply look to the imperial measurements on the left-hand side and you will see that 4mm corresponds to 5⁄32in.

If you need to convert metric dimensions into inches and you have a calculator, you can do a quick and fairly accurate conversion by using the following method:

Multiply the number of millimetres by 0.03937 to convert to inches

Multiply the number of inches by 25.4 to convert to millimetres

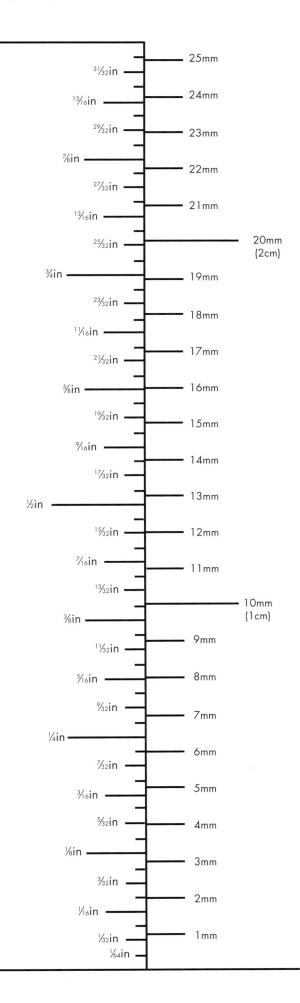

DRILL TABLE

The minidrill, as its name implies, uses small drill bits and accessories. In order to help choose the correct size of miniature drill bit for different tasks such as drilling pilot and clearance holes for the smaller screws, the table below will help you in your choice of the correct sized drill bit for the job.

SCREW GAUGE	CLEARANCE HOLE		PILOT HOLE	
	Decimal	Fraction	Decimal	Fraction
0	0.060"	1/16in	0.035"	1/32in
1	0.075"	5/64in	0.040"	1/32in
2	0.095"	5/64in	0.050"	3/64in
3	0.100"	3/32in	0.058"	1/16in
4	0.110"	7/64in	0.065"	5/32in

Miniature drill bits are supplied either singly or in sets. These may be either metric sizes which are usually available in 0.1mm. steps and sets often start with a 0.4mm drill and go on up to the maximum size the chuck of the drill can take which is often around 3.2mm. Most drill sets will contain bits in 0.2mm steps from the minimum of 0.4mm on up to the maximum. Other drill bit sets are available in the imperial equivalent sizes and often even smaller drill bits can be bought in wire gauge sizes corresponding to the numbered drill bits. The table below gives imperial/metric equivalents for some of the more popular sizes of drill bit.

IMPERIAL FRACTION	METRIC EQUIVALENT
1/64in	0.4mm
1/32in	0.8mm
3/64in	1.2mm
1/16in	1.6mm
5/64in	2.0mm
3/32in	2.4mm
7/64in	2.8mm
1/8in	3.2mm

Minidrill accessories

Tool rack

There are a great many small fixtures and fittings available for the minidrill – drill bits, burrs, grinding and cutting wheels and sanding discs. A purpose-built rack to house all the various items is a useful accessory. The rack allows you to see all the tools at a glance and quickly and easily select the right tool for the job. It also ensures that they remain clear of the dust and debris that gathers on the work bench.

The tool rack consists of two pieces of wood measuring 150 x 80mm (6 x 3¼in). The top piece has cutouts

YOU WILL NEED:

A piece of softwood such as pine of about 150mm x 80mm x 20mm (6in x 3¼in x ¾in)

A piece of MDF or ply, 7mm (¼in) thickness the same size as the pine

4 small woodscrews about no.6 x 8mm (⅝in)

Four self-adhesive feet

Plain paper

Spray mount or similar adhesive

◄ Use the paper pattern as a guide when marking out the top piece of the tool rack

to house the accessories. The bottom piece acts as a base so that items do not fall through on to the bench. The dimensions of the two pieces are not critical and can be adjusted to suit whatever range of tools you need to house. The top piece is made from pine or any other softwood offcut of around 20mm (¾in), while the bottom piece is much thinner – 7mm (¼in) and on the example shown here was made from a scrap of MDF.

1 Collect together all the drill bits, burrs and everything else you wish to include in the tool rack and lay them out on the bench to give you an idea of the finished size of item you will need to construct. The example rack shown will hold all the items supplied in a standard hobby kit. This should prove

adequate for most users, but the rack can always be made a little longer, to hold extra tools, if necessary.

2 A paper pattern is a useful cutting and drilling guide. Fine tune the hole layout to accommodate all your tools and accessories and leave space to house future additions. Adapt and copy the template at the end of this project on to plain paper.

3 Mark up the outline of the paper pattern on the wood with a pencil. Cut around this outline.

4 Use a little spray mount adhesive to stick the relevant paper patterns in place on the 20mm (¾in) wood and MDF. You now have a good, clear guide as to what each piece will look like.

▲ Use a minidrill to make the starter holes for the disc storage compartments

5 Use the minidrill to drill holes where necessary in the top piece of wood and starter holes for the cutouts which will house the cutting and grinding wheels and sanding discs. Drill all the way through; the bottom section will provide the base of the storage compartments.

6 Remove the wood from the storage compartments with a fretsaw, if you have one, or you can use a thin burr to remove the outside edges of each compartment until the starter holes join up and the waste material falls away.

7 When you have completed all the drilling and cutting, clean up the top and sides of the top piece of the tool rack with sandpaper to leave a smooth finish.

8 Use the top piece as a guide to mark a cutting line on the MDF. Cut this to size and sand the piece smooth around the edges. Drill and countersink four small pilot holes for the woodscrews which will secure the top to the bottom of the rack.

Pilot holes should be the diameter of the core of the screw without the thread. They prevent the wood from splitting as the screws are driven home.

► Use the completed top piece of the tool rack as a guide to mark out the bottom piece

14

◄ Drill the pilot holes in the bottom piece

▼ Fit the self-adhesive rubber feet in place over the fixing screws

9 Screw the bottom of the rack to the top. There is no need to use wood glue as well as there will be no stress on the rack to speak of. Four screws of about 8mm (⁵⁄₁₆in) no.6 size will be more than adequate.

10 The example shown was finished off with a set of four self-adhesive rubber feet which stop the finished tool rack from sliding about on the bench. They also cover the fixing screws giving the finished item a neater appearance.

TOOL RACK TEMPLATE

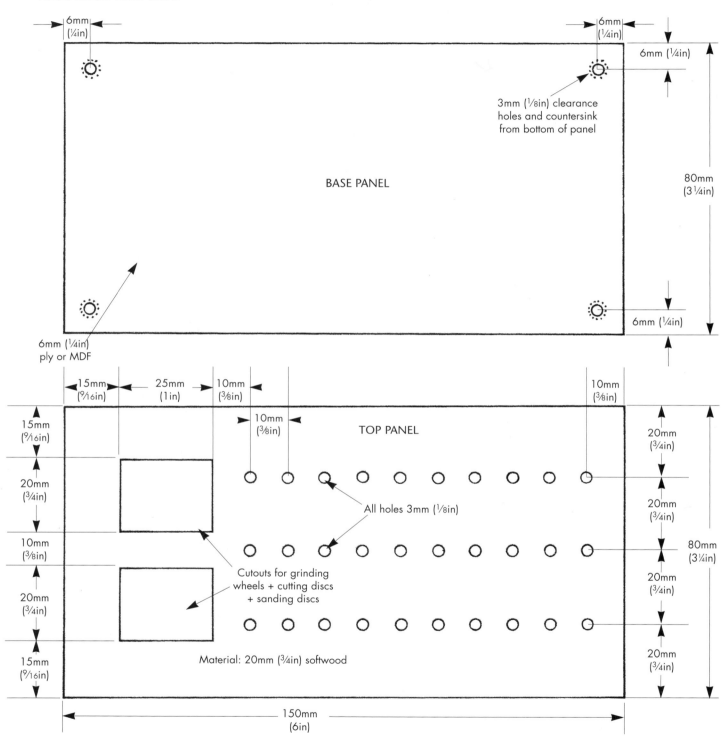

6mm (¼in)

6mm (¼in)

6mm (¼in)

3mm (⅛in) clearance holes and countersink from bottom of panel

BASE PANEL

80mm (3¼in)

6mm (¼in)

6mm (¼in) ply or MDF

15mm (⁹⁄₁₆in)

25mm (1in)

10mm (⅜in)

10mm (⅜in)

10mm (⅜in)

TOP PANEL

15mm (⁹⁄₁₆in)

20mm (¾in)

20mm (¾in)

20mm (¾in)

20mm (¾in)

20mm (¾in)

80mm (3¼in)

10mm (⅜in)

All holes 3mm (⅛in)

Cutouts for grinding wheels + cutting discs + sanding discs

20mm (¾in)

15mm (⁹⁄₁₆in)

20mm (¾in)

Material: 20mm (¾in) softwood

150mm (6in)

Drill stand

There are several projects in this book which require holes to be drilled precisely vertical. For instance, the joints of the puppet need to be exactly vertical, otherwise the limbs would not bend freely. You can usually purchase a ready-made vertical drill stand from the maker of your minidrill or you can make this one for next to nothing. It only requires a few small pieces of wood which could certainly qualify as offcuts and very little else

other than a couple of spring steel tool clips and a few screws.

The drill stand does not necessarily have to be vertical but it needs to produce drilled holes that are at a precise right angle to the workpiece. This requirement can be accomplished just as well from a horizontal position as a vertical one. By making the drill stand horizontally, you eliminate the need for costly return springs and precisely aligned columns.

YOU WILL NEED:

A piece of ply 300 x 150mm x12mm (11¾in x 6in x ½in) for the baseboard

Another piece of the same type of ply for the work table measuring 150mm x 162.5mm (6in x 6⅜in)

A piece of wood 150mm x 20mm x 45mm (11¾in x ¾in x 1¾in)

An offcut of wood 75mm x 50mm x 115mm (3in x 2in x 4½in)

2 strips of wood 175mm x 19mm x 35mm (6⅞in x ¾in x 1⅜in)

6 woodscrews about no.6 x 32mm (1¼in)

2 spring steel tool clips to suit the make and model of drill you have (one larger and one smaller)

Small piece of wood to attach to the front end of the block to level the drill

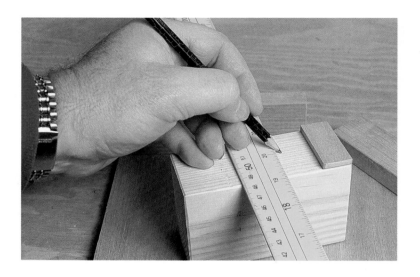

1 Make any alterations you require to the template to ensure that it suits your own type and make of drill. Use the dimensions which are given on the templates and cut the following pieces: the drill carriage, the runners, the back board, the drilling board and its brace.

Make sure that all the angles in this accessory are perfect right angles. Check the angles with a set square as you progress, adding packing pieces if they are required.

2 Mark a centre line along the drill carriage. This will give the position for the screws which will secure the spring steel tool clips to hold the drill exactly in the centre of the carriage.

3 Cut the packing piece which supports the drill at the front of the drill carriage to suit your own make. This piece will build up the height of the smaller tool clip so that the body of your drill will be precisely parallel to the drill carriage.

▲ Mark out the centre line along the middle of the piece that will become the drill carriage

▼ Screw the packing piece to the drill carriage

◄ Clip the minidrill in position at the front to allow for the accurate positioning of the back clip

▼ Mark the centre line along the base

4 Mark the centre of the packing piece and drill a clearance hole for the screw to pass through. Drill two more holes and countersink them, one on either side of the centre hole to fix the plate in position on the drill carriage. Glue and screw the packing piece down to the drill carriage. Fit and screw down the spring steel tool clip.

5 Fit the tool clip in place on the back of your drill and then clip the drill in place on the front tool clip you have just fixed. Mark the position of the fixing hole of the back tool clip. Screw the back tool clip into position on the drill carriage.

   Check that the body of the drill is parallel to the drill carriage. If it is not exactly parallel, then adjust the packing piece to suit.

► Put the drill carriage in place and accurately position the runners

▼ Check the accuracy of the runners

6 Mark out a centre line along the base. Place the drill carriage centrally over the line. Sit the two runners in place alongside the drill carriage. Mark their positions on the base with a pencil. Remove all the pieces from the base, and drill and countersink pilot holes for fixing screws for the runners on the underside of the base. One screw at each end of each runner will suffice.

7 Add a little glue to the underside of the runners and attach them to the base, fixing the screws firmly in place. Check that the drill carriage will slide easily but not sloppily between the guide rails. If the drill carriage is a little tight, then sand off a little wood from the side of the drill carriage until it glides freely between the rails.

8 Fit the support block for the back board. You need to make sure that it is at right angles, checking the angle with a square. Drill and countersink the fixing holes from underneath the base, and then glue and screw the support block in place. Check again that the support block is still at right angles to the base.

◄ Check the angle of the back board with a set square

9 Add the back board and secure it in place by screwing it to the support block. Once again, check that the work table is precisely vertical with a set square. If it is not at a precise right angle, you can add small packing pieces between the back board and the support block or shave a little wood from the support block.

10 Clip the drill to the drill carriage and slide it up towards the back board with a drill bit in place. Mark where the drill touches the back board and drill out a 6mm (¼in) hole. This ensures that the drill can pass through the material you are drilling and on into the hole in the back board without damaging the accessory itself.

▼ Use the minidrill with a drill bit fitted to mark the position of the relief hole in the back board

▲ Drill pilot holes to fit the back board to the support block with the minidrill

DRILL STAND TEMPLATE Side elevation

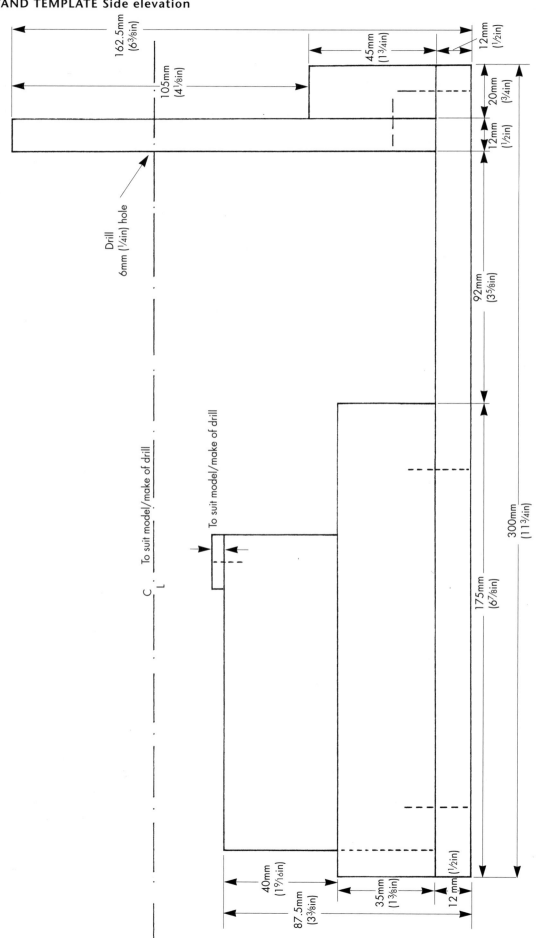

162.5mm (6³⁄₈in)

105mm (4¹⁄₈in)

45mm (1³⁄₄in)

12mm (¹⁄₂in)

20mm (³⁄₄in)

12mm (¹⁄₂in)

92mm (3⁵⁄₈in)

300mm (11³⁄₄in)

175mm (6⁷⁄₈in)

Drill 6mm (¹⁄₄in) hole

To suit model/make of drill

To suit model/make of drill

C L

40mm (1⁹⁄₁₆in)

87.5mm (3³⁄₈in)

35mm (1³⁄₈in)

12 mm (¹⁄₂in)

12 mm (¹⁄₂in)

DRILL STAND TEMPLATE Plan view

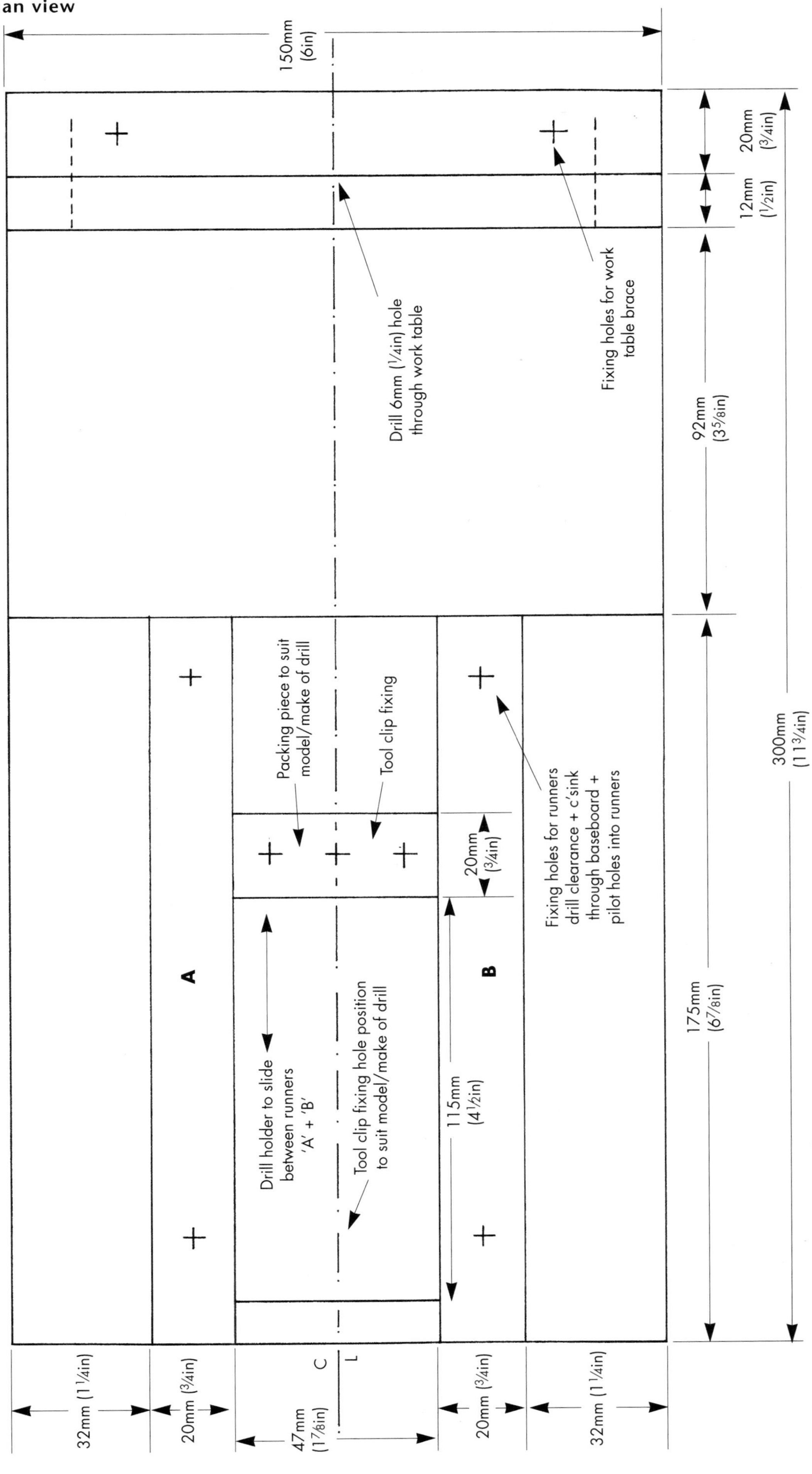

150mm (6in)

20mm (3/4in)

12mm (1/2in)

92mm (3 5/8in)

300mm (11 3/4in)

Drill 6mm (1/4in) hole through work table

Fixing holes for work table brace

Packing piece to suit model/make of drill

Tool clip fixing

A

B

20mm (3/4in)

Fixing holes for runners drill clearance + c'sink through baseboard + pilot holes into runners

Drill holder to slide between runners 'A' + 'B'

Tool clip fixing hole position to suit model/make of drill

115mm (4 1/2in)

175mm (6 7/8in)

32mm (1 1/4in)

20mm (3/4in)

47mm (1 7/8in)

C

L

20mm (3/4in)

32mm (1 1/4in)

Lathe attachment

The lathe attachment is simply an additional tool rest which fits in place alongside the chuck of the drill to permit the shaping of small items that can be held in the chuck of the minidrill. Some of the manufacturers of minidrills include a small face plate in their range of accessories, by gluing your workpiece on to such a device, you can carry out turning and shaping operations on larger items than would otherwise fit into the chuck directly. If

you manage to split the workpiece from the face plate, you are applying too much pressure to the tool in use.

The main requirement of this accessory is that the drill remains perfectly parallel to the baseboard and is held securely in place. You can decide

YOU WILL NEED:

Baseboard of 12mm (1/2in) ply measuring 270mm x 225mm (10 1/2in x 9in)

Support block made from an offcut of 75mm x 50mm (3in x 2in), 115mm (4 1/2in) in length

Offcut of thin sheet material to make packing piece to ensure drill is parallel to the support block (if necessary)

2 pieces of wood to hold the drill in place, 20mm x 20mm x 20mm (3/4in x 3/4in x 3/4in)

2 check support blocks, 50mm x 20mm x 20mm (2in x 3/4in x 3/4in), and 55mm x 20mm x 20mm (2 3/16in x 3/4in x 3/4in)

6mm x 35mm (1/4in x 1 3/8in) cheesehead screw with plain washer and wing nut

Woodscrews

2 clips to fit your drill (a pipe clip and a tool clip were used here)

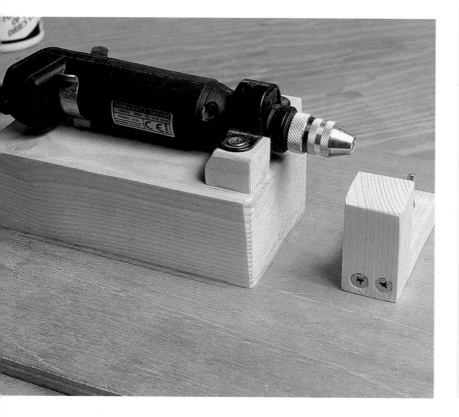

to make just the horizontal drill stand if you wish and leave out the tool rest addition. If so, then you will not need the screw or the two pieces of wood that form the tool rest. You can always add this part of the accessory at a later date if you want to.

1 Check the dimensions of your minidrill and modify the template accordingly. Use the template to cut out the pieces. Mark the centre of the chuck support blocks which will hold the drill in place by drawing diagonal lines. Mark the placement of these blocks on the drill support block, checking that they will fit your make and model of minidrill.

▼ Fit the main support block to the baseboard with wood glue and four no.6 x 32mm (1¼in) screws

2 Mark out a centre line on the baseboard and a centre line on the bottom of the support block. Use the line to position the support block on the baseboard. You may need to make up a small packing piece to ensure that the minidrill is parallel to the support block. Glue and screw the support block on to the baseboard. For the example shown here, no.6 x 32mm (1¼in) screws were used.

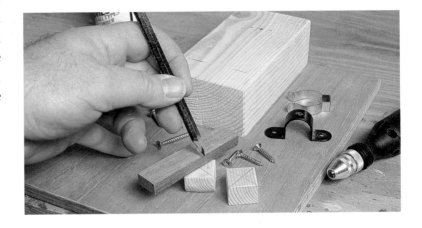

▲ Mark out the centres of the chuck support

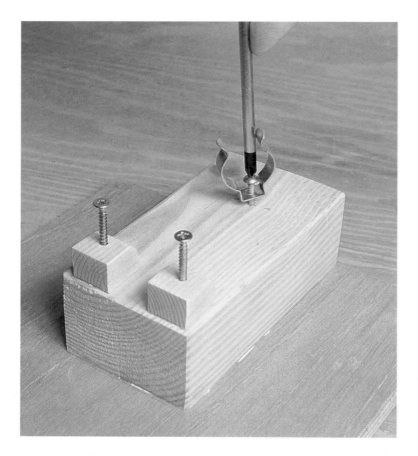

3 Drill pilot holes in the centre of the two chuck support blocks. Glue the chuck support blocks in place at the front of the support block, which will hold the drill in place. Screw the tool clip in place at the back of the support block, checking that it provides a good tight fit around the body of your drill and does not allow it to slip around under light pressure. Screw the front pipe clip into place on the chuck support blocks.

With the drill held firmly in place, you can now carry out shaping and sanding operations with both hands free to hold the workpiece, which will result in much safer operation and much greater accuracy.

◄ Fit the tool clip in place on the support block to clamp the body of the minidrill in place

► The minidrill held securely in place with a pipe clip and tool clip, ready for use as a basic horizontal drill stand

ADDING THE TOOL REST

4 Fix the two pieces which make up the tool rest in place using the template as a guide. Check the height needed for the tool rest on the lathe attachment against a drill bit held in the chuck of the drill. The tool rest needs to be at about the centrepoint of the drill bit for a cutting tool to be in the correct position for cutting. The photograph (see right) shows how to join and shape the tool rest wood and fit the pieces together.

5 The tool rest is fixed in place with a cheesehead screw which is threaded through the baseboard and secured underneath the stand with a wingnut. Drill a 6mm (¼in) hole through the baseboard at each end of where the slot needs to be and join up the two holes with a padsaw. Turn the baseboard over and using a burr, remove enough material along the sides of the slot for the head of the 6mm (¼in) screw to slide along without protruding below the level of the baseboard.

6 The tool rest can be easily added on or removed to alter the purpose of the minidrill accessory.

▲ Assembling the tool rest

◄ Milling the recess for the head of the locking screw with a burr

◄ Fitting the tool rest in place with a plain washer and wingnut

LATHE ATTACHMENT BASIC UNIT TEMPLATE

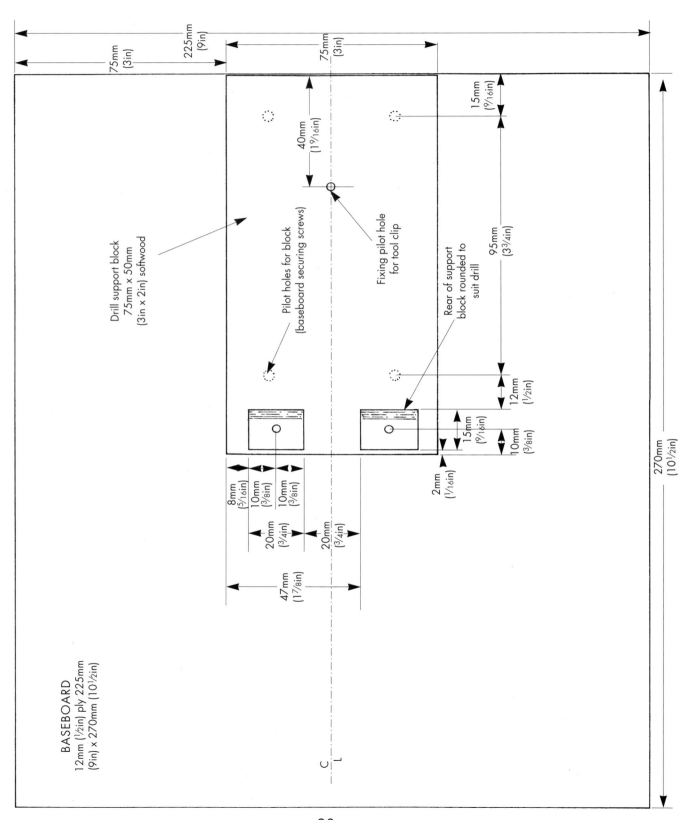

BASEBOARD
12mm (½in) ply 225mm
(9in) x 270mm (10½in)

Drill support block
75mm x 50mm
(3in x 2in) softwood

Pilot holes for block
(baseboard securing screws)

Fixing pilot hole
for tool clip

Rear of support
block rounded to
suit drill

75mm
(3in)

225mm
(9in)

75mm
(3in)

40mm
(1⁹⁄₁₆in)

15mm
(⁹⁄₁₆in)

95mm
(3³⁄₄in)

12mm
(½in)

15mm
(⁹⁄₁₆in)

10mm
(³⁄₈in)

2mm
(¹⁄₁₆in)

270mm
(10½in)

8mm
(⁵⁄₁₆in)

10mm
(³⁄₈in)

10mm
(³⁄₈in)

20mm
(³⁄₄in)

20mm
(³⁄₄in)

47mm
(1⁷⁄₈in)

CL

LATHE ATTACHMENT TOOL REST TEMPLATE

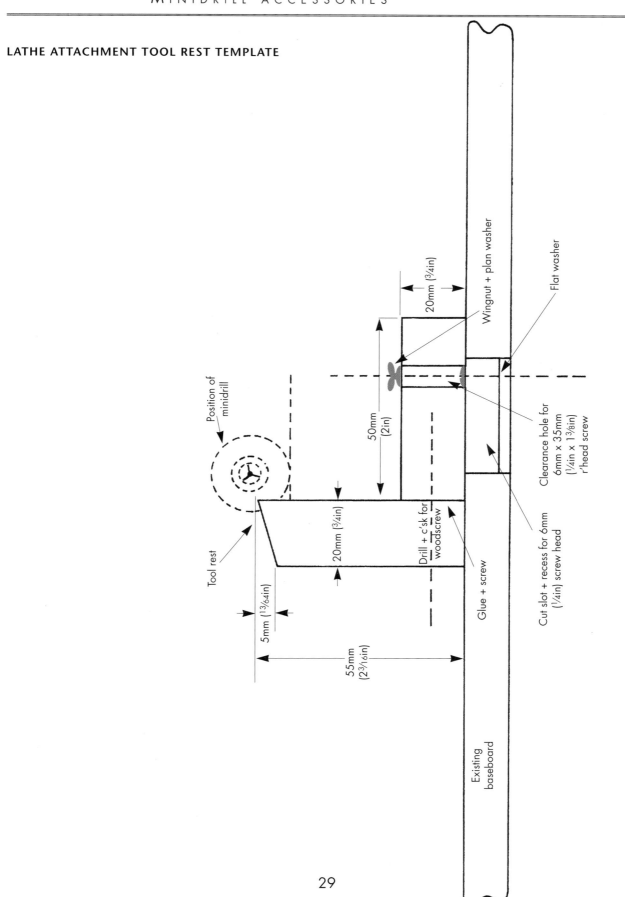

Position of minidrill

Tool rest

Wingnut + plan washer

Flat washer

20mm (¾in)

50mm (2in)

20mm (¾in)

Drill + c'sk for woodscrew

5mm (¹³⁄₆₄in)

55mm (2³⁄₁₆in)

Glue + screw

Cut slot + recess for 6mm (¼in) screw head

Clearance hole for 6mm x 35mm (¼in x 1³⁄₈in) r'head screw

Existing baseboard

Router table

The router consists of an open-sided box made from 12mm (½in) ply, held together with plastic assembly blocks of the type much used in kitchen cabinets and self-assembly furniture. A sliding drill plate allows the minidrill to be moved up and down to alter the

YOU WILL NEED:

12mm (½in) ply to make the following panels:

200mm x 190mm (8in x 7½in, two of these will be required

190mm x 150mm (7½in x 6in)

110mm x 95mm (4⁵⁄₁₆in x 3¾in)

255mm x 200mm (10in x 8in), two of these will be needed

Hardwood strip measuring 255mm x 32mm (10in x 1¼in)

4 x 6mm (¼in) x 32mm (1¼in) machine screws with plain washers and wing nuts to suit

12 plastic assembly blocks with no.6 x 20mm (¾in) woodscrews to suit (you will need 3 screws per assembly block)

2 spring steel tool clips and appropriate screws (check that these fit your make and model of minidrill)

This accessory is particularly useful for making miniature boxes, dolls' houses and many other items where routing is required on a small scale. This miniature router has a sturdy, yet simple design which is inexpensive to produce with even the most basic of workshop facilities. It will allow you to clip your minidrill in and out with ease. You will be able to use full range of burrs as miniature routers on a wide range of materials.

position of the burr and a sliding router fence allows accurate positioning of the workpiece. There are other fixtures which can be used with this router table. If you are particularly interested in this area refer to a standard work on routers for the appropriate designs which can be copied down to size for use with the minidrill.

1 Measure and cut out all the panels of wood required. Refer to the templates, carefully measuring your minidrill to check that the dimensions given are correct for your model. Make any adaptations necessary.

2 Start by making up the drill plate. This is made from the panel of 12mm (½in) ply which measures 110 x 95mm (4⁵⁄₁₆ x 3¾in). Position and screw in the rear spring steel tool clip. Clip the minidrill into the rear clip, then clip the tool clip intended to fix the front of the drill in place even though it is not yet attached to the drill plate.

3 Check that the body of the drill is level and parallel with the plate. Measure the gap at the front of the drill between the bottom of the tool clip and the drill plate. Make up a thin piece of wood to place between the bottom of the tool clip and the drill plate to ensure that the drill remains perfectly parallel to the plate. Drill through the packing piece and screw through the tool clip, the packing piece and into the drill plate. Use a little wood glue between the packing piece and the drill plate for added security.

It is important to make sure the cutting head of the router is exactly vertical. It may not matter much with some shapes of burr or router, but it certainly will with straight-sided ones.

4 The drill plate has two slots cut into it along each of the longer sides. This allows the minidrill to slide up and down, varying the position of the cutting burr. The slots will take 6mm (¼in) machine screws. Don't make the slots too wide or it will be difficult to maintain accuracy when using the router table. Drill a 6mm (¼in) clearance hole at each end as marked on the template and simply join them with a pencil line, then cut out the slot with a pad saw or fretsaw. Cut a recess in the slot to allow the screw heads to sit below the surface of the back of the drill plate.

▼ The minidrill positioned on the drill plate to check that the body of the drill is parallel

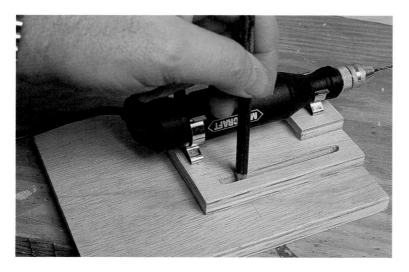

6 Take one of the 255 x 200mm (10 x 8in) pieces of 12mm (½in) ply and mark it up for the slots down each side. Check the position of these using the template. These are of the same type and dimension as you have already made for the drill plate. Drill 20mm (¾in) holes inside the cutout shape with a wood bit. Cut down from the edge of the panel with an appropriate saw.

▲ Once the slots have been cut in the drill plate mark the positions for the screws on the back panel of the router table

5 Mark the position of the securing screws through the drill plate on the back panel. Drill the two 6mm (¼in) holes for the screws which will attach the drill plate to the back panel. The template shows where you should locate these holes.

The top plate contains a keyhole-shape cutout at the front of the panel. This is for the shaft of the burr or bit. The cutout may seem a little large, but it may have to accommodate miniature routing bits as well as tiny burrs.

7 Make the slots down the sides of the top plate in the same way as you did for the drill plate. These slots are slightly longer so that they can accommodate a wide variety of workpiece sizes. Check the width of the slots by inserting a machine screw and sliding it the length of the slot, making sure that it runs freely.

8 To make the fence, take the hardwood strip. Put the strip of hardwood over the top plate and mark holes corresponding to the slots in the top plate. Drill appropriate clearance holes for the 6 x 32mm (¼ x 1¼in) machine screws.

A router fence allows you to cut the correct amount of material evenly from the workpiece. You can move the fence forward a little to make subsequent cuts, so that you can remove the material in stages causing less strain on the drill and creating a clean finish.

▼ The completed drill plate in position on the back panel

9 You should be left with three panels – the two side panels and the base panel. You will notice that the base panel is the same size as the top panel, and that the side panels sit inside the edges of the top and base panels. The slots for the router fence on the top panel are outside the side panels which allows uninterrupted adjustment of the fence. The bottom panel is the same size so that the edges will protrude beyond the uprights, allowing the router table to be clamped to a workbench.

10 Assemble the side and back panels between the top and base panels, making sure that everything remains square. Once the assembly block screws have all been tightened, fit your minidrill and check that it slides well and clears the keyhole cutout on the top panel. Make sure that

the chuck of the minidrill clears the keyhole cutout. If there is a small discrepancy, unscrew the drill plate from the back panel and add a thin packing sheet.

▲ Fit the assembly blocks to the panels which make up the framework of the router table

◄ The router table ready for fitting the minidrill. Note the router fence on the top panel which can be adjusted in the same way as the height of the drill to ensure accuracy in the actual routing operation

33

ROUTER TABLE TEMPLATE

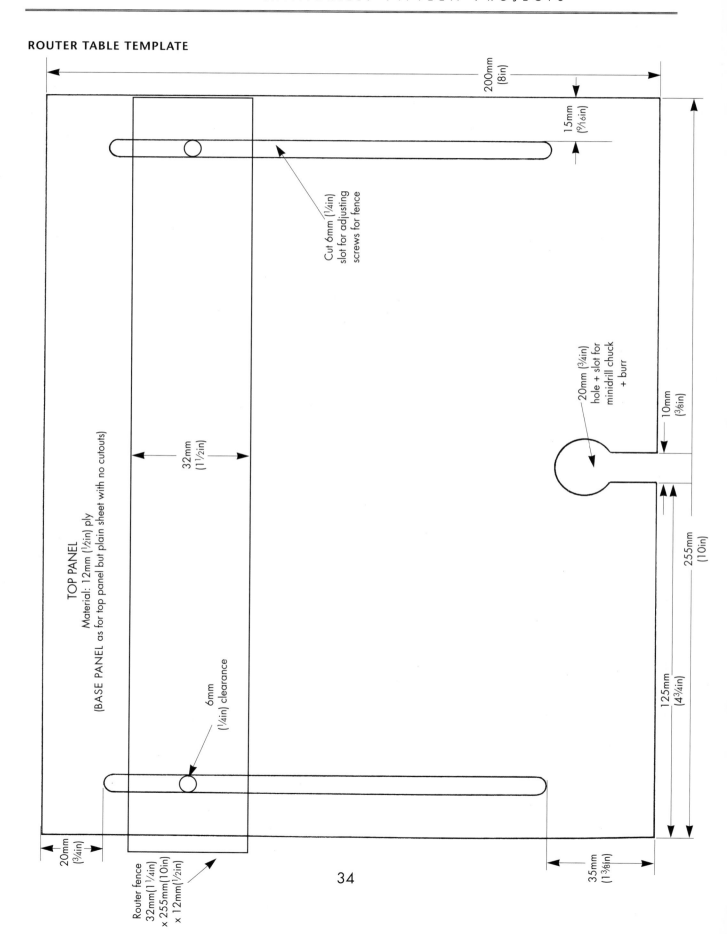

200mm (8in)

15mm (⁹⁄₁₆in)

Cut 6mm (¼in) slot for adjusting screws for fence

20mm (¾in) hole + slot for minidrill chuck + burr

10mm (³⁄₈in)

255mm (10in)

125mm (4¾in)

35mm (1³⁄₈in)

32mm (1½in)

TOP PANEL
Material: 12mm (½in) ply
(BASE PANEL as for top panel but plain sheet with no cutouts)

6mm (¼in) clearance

20mm (¾in)

Router fence
32mm(1¼in)
x 255mm(10in)
x 12mm(½in)

ROUTER TABLE TEMPLATE

SIDE SUPPORT PANELS
Cut 2 Material: 12mm (½in) ply
BASE PANEL – not shown Material: 12mm (½in) ply
size 200mm x 255mm (8in x 10in)

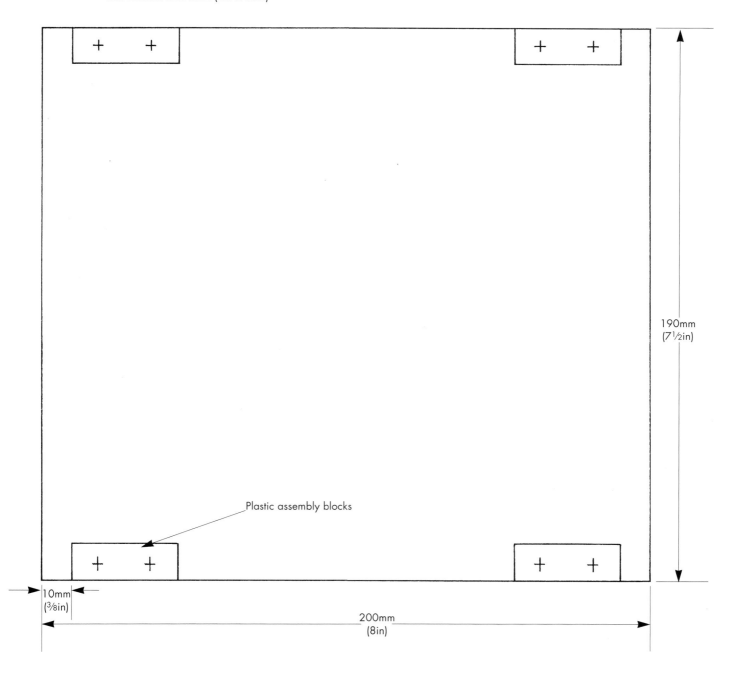

Plastic assembly blocks

190mm
(7½in)

10mm
(⅜in)

200mm
(8in)

DRILL PLATE TEMPLATE

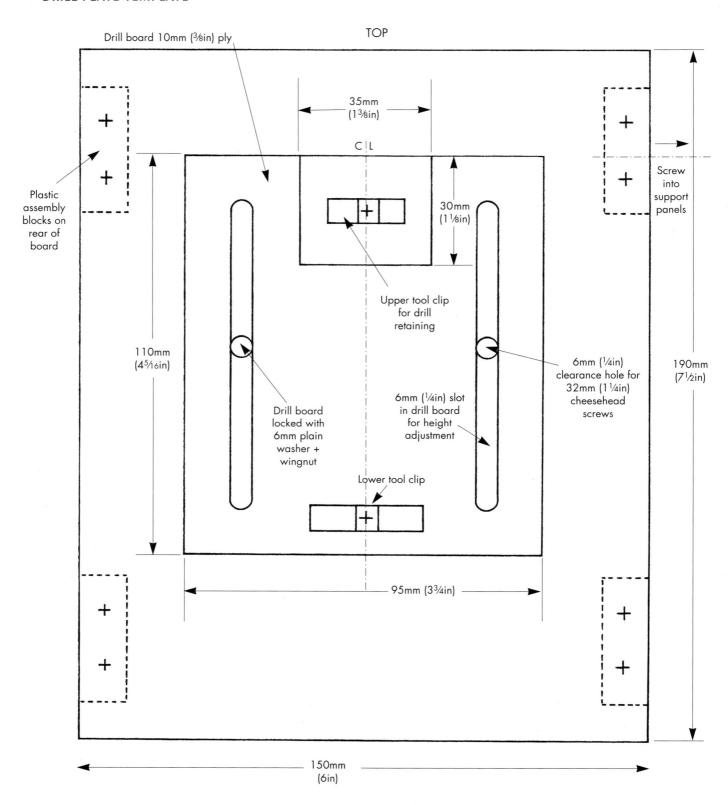

Drill board 10mm (⅜in) ply

TOP

35mm (1⅜in)

C⏐L

Plastic assembly blocks on rear of board

Screw into support panels

30mm (1⅛in)

Upper tool clip for drill retaining

110mm (4⁵⁄₁₆in)

6mm (¼in) clearance hole for 32mm (1¼in) cheesehead screws

190mm (7½in)

Drill board locked with 6mm plain washer + wingnut

6mm (¼in) slot in drill board for height adjustment

Lower tool clip

95mm (3¾in)

150mm (6in)

Engraving projects

Engraved mirror

You can use any size or shape of mirror you want for this type of project. The design for the engraving can be enlarged or reduced to suit your requirements. You can also use almost any pen-and-ink drawing or old engraving. There should not be any shortage of originals to copy or adapt for the purpose. Be careful of copyright restrictions, but if the item is only for your own use, then there should be no problems.

Decide what mirror you intend to use for the project. If you have a spare one to hand all well and good, but they can be bought quite cheaply from many bargain stores. Mirrors are even available ready framed, so if you see one of these that you like and can remove and refit the frame easily after you have finished engraving the mirror, then it will certainly be suitable for your project.

YOU WILL NEED:

A mirror

White paper or tracing paper, to make the pattern

Engraving tool or engraving point, suitable for your minidrill

White paint – poster paint, emulsion or acrylic

Carbon paper

1 Make a copy of the design you want to engrave on a sheet of plain white paper. Use tracing paper if you find this easier. Trace the main outlines and major details within the design. You can copy the finer detail later directly from the original.

◄ The mirror, the pattern and carbon paper ready to start work

3 Cover the glass with carbon paper put face down. Then position the pattern you intend to engrave. Using a suitable point, a fairly blunt pencil or a ballpoint pen which has run out of ink, draw over the outlines of the drawing so that an impression is formed through the carbon paper onto the coat of white paint below. Do not be afraid to use a ruler to help you with accuracy if straight lines are involved, such as the masts of the fishing boats in the example used here.

4 Remove the drawing and the carbon paper. Fit an engraving point into your minidrill or engraving pen. Begin engraving on the lines nearest to your dominant hand, so that you do not rub away the carbon paper lines as you work. The engraving point will cut right through the coat of paint and into the surface of the glass with no difficulty. You will not need to apply much pressure to the engraving point.

▲ Apply a coat of white poster paint to the surface of the mirror to provide both a background for the carbon paper impression of the picture detail and to deaden any reflections

2 Clean the glass of the mirror and give it a coat of white paint. This will stop the mirror from reflecting and provide a suitable base for engraving. The coat of white paint will form a good background for the carbon paper impression.

▶ Trace through the carbon paper with an empty ball point pen to produce a copy of the main lines of the picture on to the coat of white paint underneath

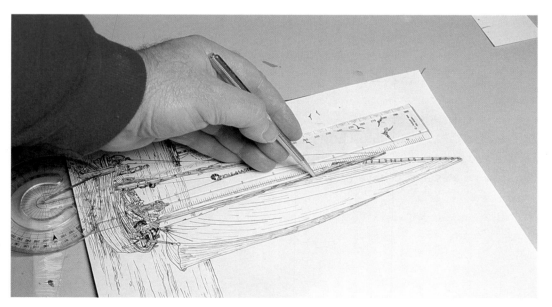

◄ Remove the white paint so that the finer detail can be added

5 Once you are happy with the amount of detail you have on the main part of the drawing, you can wipe off the coat of white paint with fine wire wool. Add the finer details using the picture as a guide. If large areas of shading are needed, change to a grinding wheel. This will cover ground quickly and easily. A grinding wheel with a flat top and a steep cone shape which tapers towards the chuck will be best for shading defined areas.

6 Carefully check over your engraving and make any final additions you need and then give the surface of the glass a good clean with almost anything really – use window cleaner, washing-up liquid or whatever you have that won't leave a smear when you have finished cleaning. Your engraved mirror is now ready to frame and hang according to your own choice.

TIP

If there are straight or fairly straight lines in the design, such as the masts on the fishing boats and the rigging lines on the picture used here, use a strip of straight wood as a guide for your engraver.

▼ Complete the fine detail of the scene before finishing off

ENGRAVED MIRROR DESIGN

Wine glasses

This project can be carried out with an engraving pen or a minidrill fitted with an engraving bit in its chuck. Apart from the wine glasses, you will need a line drawing or an engraving to copy on to the glass. The ones shown here were adapted from some nineteenth-century engravings so that they form a wraparound design on the bowl of the glass.

When you make your copy, draw it on the thinnest paper you can as it will need to bend easily. Use the designs given by way of example here, if you like, or choose one of your own which have illustrations that appeal to you.

Whatever picture you choose to engrave on to your glasses, make sure that the picture will fit well in the glass bowl; photocopy up or down to size as appropriate.

1 Make a copy of the design you have chosen. Cut out the pictures so that there is no waste paper left around the actual design itself. This will help you to form the picture around the inside of the bowl of the glass without too many creases in the paper. Once you have the picture in place and have aligned it to suit the effect you require, lightly tape the picture in place so that it will not move around.

2 Make some form of support for the glass and a rest for your hand while you are doing the actual engraving. Although you only need a fairly light touch to accomplish the engraving, if your designs are anything other than the simplest outline, your hand will begin to tire if left unsupported. A couple of blocks of wood and a panel make an effective temporary hand rest. The blocks of wood need to allow the panel of wood to clear the glasses so the size of these blocks will depend on the dimensions of the glasses.

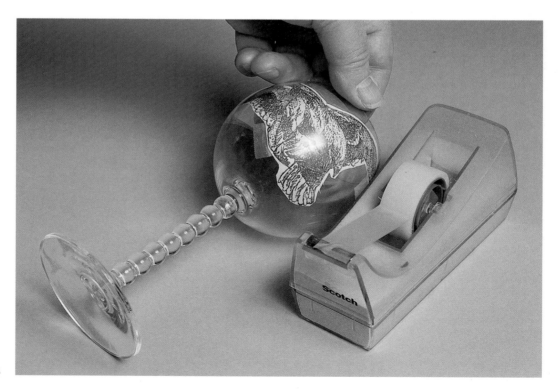

► Tape the pattern in place to make a wraparound design on the glass

◄ Use the original packaging to support the glasses with support blocks and a hand rest panel ready to be put in place

▼ Follow the paper pattern with the engraving tool fitted with a diamond engraving point

3 Fit a diamond or tungsten carbide engraving point in either your engraving tool or minidrill. Begin by engraving the main outlines of the pictures you have chosen, then add the details. Use a grinding wheel to cover large areas of shading. Most engraving kits include a couple of different shapes of grinding wheel for this very purpose.

4 Once you have completed the engraving, remove the original patterns and check your work against the light. You may find that there are details you wish to correct or add to once you have seen your engraving on its own without the pattern in place. When you are happy with the results, give each glass a good clean and enjoy the results of your efforts.

ENGRAVED WINE GLASS DESIGNS

Acrylic signs

Acrylic sheet material is widely available in most DIY stores in a variety of thicknesses. It is ideal for making signs with the minidrill fitted with an engraving point. There are many uses for signs in and around the house, for business and many other applications. To have them made up professionally can be expensive, particularly if you happen to need quite a few of them.

The actual acrylic sheet is usually available in 2mm (1/16in) and 4mm (5/32in) thicknesses. The 4mm (5/32in) thick version is a better option as it tends to be more rigid. The 2mm (1/16in)

YOU WILL NEED:

Minidrill with engraving point or engraving pen

Craft knife

Steel ruler

Acrylic sheet in whatever thickness you decide on

Sheet of paper

Lettering and numerals as appropriate to the sign you wish to make

Finishing materials such as a frame, keyring or chain

type can also be used and is probably better suited to signs that will ultimately be attached a door or fitted into a frame. The engraving technique is the same for either type. This material is easy to cut to the required size. The sheet usually comes with a protective film on both surfaces to protect it from scratching. Mark out the size you need and score along the lines a few times with a sharp craft knife on both sides of the sheet and simply snap it off.

1 Decide what size and shape you want your sign to be. Draw the shape you require on to the protective covering of the acrylic sheet with a marker pen. Put the acrylic sheet on a piece of scrap board such as ply or hardboard, to protect your work surface while you are cutting. Score along the line you have drawn with a craft knife. Do not press too hard on

the knife. It is better to use several strokes of the knife if necessary to effect a sufficiently deep score line.

2 Turn the sheet over and score the other side along the same line. You will be able to see through to the first score line as the protective film is virtually transparent. With both sides of the sheet suitably scored with the craft knife, you will be able to snap off the section you have marked easily. Use your ruler as a guide to make doubly sure that the acrylic sheet will not be inclined to snap off in the wrong place.

3 The scored edges of the acrylic sheet will be a little rough and uneven. Gently rub along them on both sides with a piece of fine sandpaper to remove the roughness before you attempt to remove the protective film from the sheet. Remove the protective film on one side.

▼ Peel off the protective layer on one side of the acrylic sheet, leaving the transparent layer in place on the other side

4 Using a plain sheet of paper, mark a baseline then trace the appropriate lettering along it. Trace the lettering from the alphabets shown here, or use lettering of your own to produce the pattern for your sign. Lay the acrylic sheet in position over the paper pattern making sure it is square to the lettering. You should be able to see the lettering through the acrylic sheet without any difficulty.

5 Set up your minidrill or engraving tool with an engraving point. Secure your acrylic sheet in place above the lettering on your tracing. This is best done with a couple of strips of tape, one on either side of the sheet, so that the acrylic sheet cannot move.

6 Take the engraving point and trace around the edges of each letter or numeral. Engrave straight edges using a strip of straight wood as a guide. Use a piece of wood which is slightly thicker than the exposed length of the engraving point so that it does not foul the engraver and create problems that way. A ruler may catch on the engraving point and could cause it to wander off its intended course.

▲ Use a strip of wood slightly thicker than the engraving point to ensure that the straight portions of the lettering are true

▼ The completed lettering outlines

TIP

It is important to keep the tracing and acrylic perfectly still while you trace the outline with the engraving point or the whole sign would be spoiled.

7 When the outlines are complete, fill in the lettering. Use light strokes of the engraving point and keep the point moving on the sheet. Follow the example shown here for the letter infilling and make all the shading lines in one direction, or use what is known as cross hatching, which is a set of lines in one direction and then another set at right angles to them. If you are not sure which method would work best, try them out on a scrap piece of acrylic sheet before you begin on your sign.

8 Once the engraving is complete, you will find that the edges of the acrylic around each letter is raised up and rough in texture. This is due to the speed and heat of the engraving point. The acrylic is soft enough to be simply removed with a finger nail without scratching the remaining acrylic.

▲ Fill in the individual letters with horizontal strokes of the engraving tool

◄ Use a thumb nail to remove the burrs thrown up by the engraving operation

◄ Engrave initials onto a small acrylic blank to make a key fob

TIP

The engraving point is moving at high speed and if it remains too long in one place it would cause the acrylic to melt, clogging the engraving point.

FINISHING AND DISPLAYING SIGNS

A small keyring fob has been produced in exactly the same way as the larger sign and after engraving, was drilled to accept a keyring fitting.

Once you have completed a sign similar to the name plate, you will find that if held in the right way the lettering appears to be lit from behind. This effect can be further exploited by framing the sign and adding a miniature fluorescent tube along one side, so that the light from the tube shines up onto the acrylic sheet. When lit, the lettering will show up as if suspended in space.

Some signs need a frame, while others may be suspended by a length of chain which can be bought from hobby or jewellery suppliers. When drilling the holes to attach a chain, slow your minidrill right down or the acrylic sheet will overheat. If your drill does not have speed control, then drill a little at a time using a very gentle pressure until you drill right through the material.

ACRYLIC SIGN DESIGNS

EXIT

A B C D E F G H I
J K L M N O P Q R
S T U V W X Y Z

1 2 3 4 5 6 7 8 9 0

a b c d e f g h i
j k l m n o p q r
s t u v w x y z

THE COTTAGE

A B C D E F
G H I J K L
M N O P Q
R S T U V
W X Y Z

ABCDEFG
HIJKLMN
OPQRSTU
VWXYZ

1234567890

abcdef
ghijklm
nopqrst
uvwxyz

54

Toy and game projects

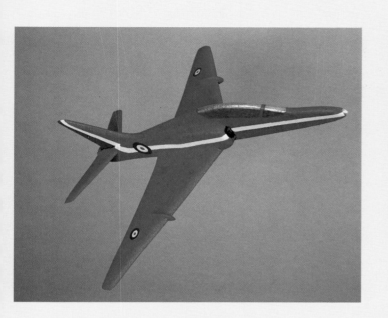

Sailing boat

YOU WILL NEED:

197mm (7¾in) length of 50 x 50mm (2 x 2in) softwood

Thin dowel for the masts (the handles of a couple of cheap artist's brushes are ideal)

Jewellery findings, some ring pins and jump rings

A couple of small pieces of cloth, to make the sails

Dual-epoxy resin and wood glue

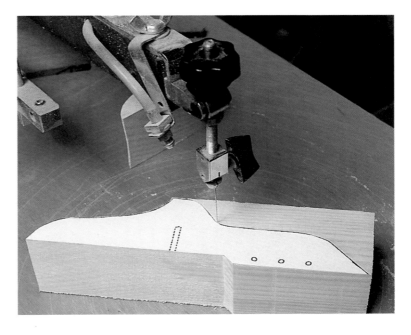

This project makes an ideal toy boat for either a paddling pool or the bath. The hull is carved with the minidrill from a length of 50 x 50mm (2 x 2in) timber and will suit an offcut from a building job as there are no special requirements for this part of the project. The little sailboat is ketch rigged with a foresail and a mainsail.

▲ Use a power scrollsaw to make the first hull cut

▼ Put the waste pieces back in place under the hull shape ready for the second cut on the hull

1 Make two patterns for the hull, one side view, one plan view, using the templates given. Then, glue the paper pattern in place on the block of 50 x 50mm (2 x 2in). Use a scrollsaw, jigsaw, or even a padsaw to cut around the shape of the pattern. Put the offcuts to one side. These will support the hull making it easier for you to make the second cut.

2 Temporarily stick the first waste bits back in place and glue the deck plan into position, making sure it is straight. Cut around the edges of the deck. Remove all the waste pieces and discard them.

3 Mark a centre line down the underside of the hull with a pencil. This will give you a point of reference when carving out the shape of the underside of the hull. Fit a disc sander into your minidrill and clamp the hull

▲ Pencil in a centre line as a carving guide for shaping the hull

▼ Use a disc sander in the minidrill to carry out the final shaping of the hull

4 Once you are happy with the general shape of the hull, drill the hole for the mast. Select a drill bit which will ensure a reasonably tight fit for the dowel you have selected to serve as a mast. Drill about halfway through the hull as shown on the template.

▲ The undercoated hull suspended on a pencil to dry

section securely. You are now ready to begin carving. Be careful with the disc sander as it will remove material surprisingly quickly. Simply shape from the deck level down to the pencil centre line rounding it off slightly. The hull should be sharper towards the bow (front), and rounder towards the stern (back) of the boat.

5 Find a heavy weight to act as a support – a reel of solder was used here – and paint the hull section with an undercoat of white primer/sealer. You can rest the hull to dry by sticking a pencil or a piece of dowelling into the mast hole and suspending the sailboat in the centre of the reel of solder – or whatever else you have acquired for the purpose.

Once the undercoat is fully dry, you are ready to complete the decoration of the hull using your own choice of colour scheme.

7 Fit your minidrill into the bench stand with the disc sander in the chuck. Sand off the dowel for the bowsprit so it sits at the correct angle on the foredeck. Remove your minidrill and refit the 0.4mm (¹⁄₆₄in) drill bit and make the hole in the bowsprit for attaching the front of the foresail. Fit ring pins for retaining the sails and the masts by smearing a light coating of dual-epoxy resin around the shaft of the ring pin before pushing it home into its pre-drilled hole.

6 Glue the mast in place and allow the glue to set fully. Once the glue has set, fit a 0.4mm (¹⁄₆₄in) drill bit in your minidrill and make the holes for the ring pins in the main mast and in the hull where the ring pins for the rigging and securing the masts will go (refer to the template). Be careful to make these holes central, particularly in the mast. Don't let the drill bit wander off line, particularly at the outset of your drilling.

▲ Drill a 0.4mm (¹⁄₆₄in) hole in the top of the main mast ready for the ring pin

8 For the ring pins which appear on both sides of a mast, such as the one at the top which holds the foresail on one side and the mainsail top mast on the other, use a single ring pin. Push the ring pin right through the hole then bend the shaft into a ring on the other side of the hole with a pair of miniature pointed-nose pliers. If you don't have suitable pliers, then just drill two holes and fit two ring pins.

◄ Use a disc sander with the minidrill clamped in the drill stand to shape the underside of the bowsprit

► Use a pair of miniature pointed-nose pliers to make another ring at the shaft end of the ring pin

9 Fit more ring pins in position on each of the two mainsail masts as shown on the template and open the rings out a little once the glue has completely set. Fit the rings through the corresponding ones on the main mast and then close the rings up again with a pair of pliers. This will allow the main sail to tack from side to side once all the rigging is in place. The securing rigging for this is a thread running through the ring below the bottom mast but not tied, and fastened to a ring pin on either side of the deck.

10 The sails are just small shapes of cotton material with the edges turned over into a hem with a thread running through each fold over. Leave plenty of spare thread at each end so the sails can be easily attached to the appropriate ring pins. Tie the sails in place on their ring pins and secure each knot with a blob of dual-epoxy resin.

► Use a wooden cocktail stick to add a blob of dual-epoxy resin adhesive to seal all the knots in the rigging

MODEL SAILING BOAT
General layout

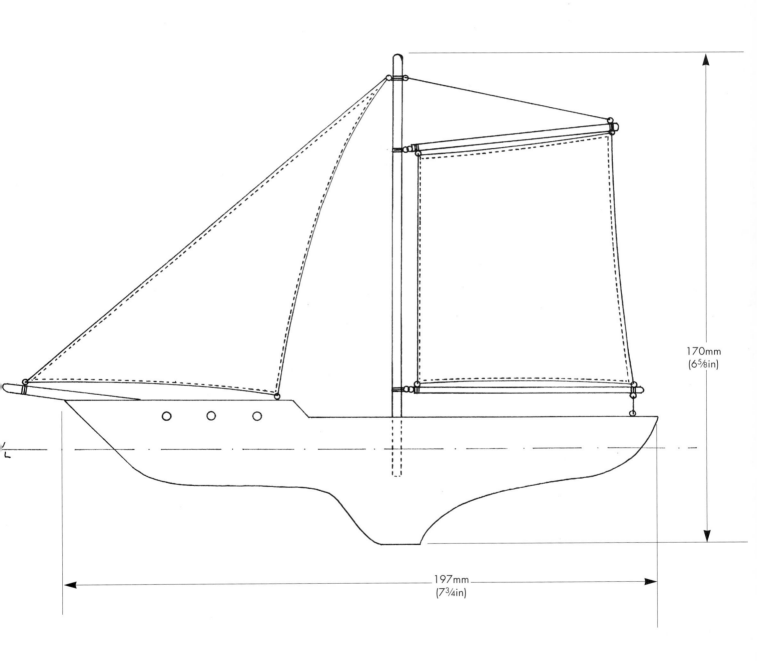

170mm
(6⅝in)

197mm
(7¾in)

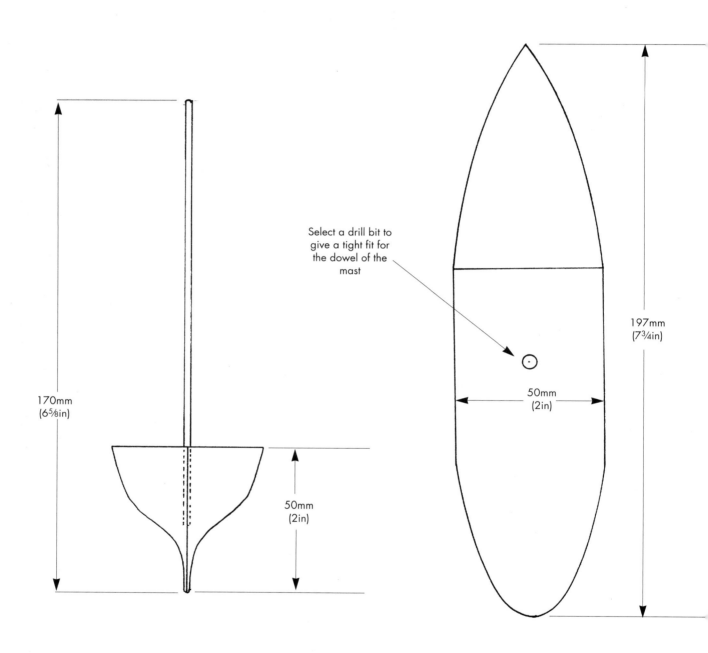

Select a drill bit to
give a tight fit for
the dowel of the
mast

197mm
(7¾in)

170mm
(6⅝in)

50mm
(2in)

50mm
(2in)

Aeroplane

This little model airplane is made from balsa wood panels, which can be bought in packs from any model or hobby shop. You will need a variety of thicknesses of panel for the various components of the aircraft, all of which are available in a standard model pack.

The aircraft will fly when it is completed and can be launched with the aid of a catapult consisting of an elastic band on top of a small piece of dowel for best results. It can also be launched by hand. This is probably best if the plane is intended as a gift for a young child. A little balancing will be required once the plane is completed but this will be outlined later on.

1 Make up a set of paper patterns from the templates, then stick the paper patterns down on the correct thickness of balsa panel with spray mount adhesive. The wings are made from 5mm (¹³⁄₆₄in) balsa, the tailplane and two wing airflow control plates are made from 3mm (⅛in) balsa, a fuselage cut from a 6mm (¼in) panel and two engine nacelles from the 10mm (⅜in) sheet.

► Use a sharp craft knife to cut out the panels

64

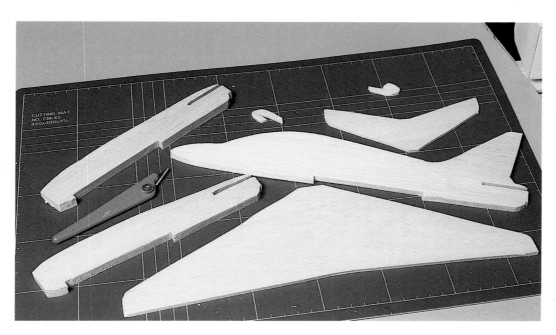

◄ The parts of the model aircraft cut out and ready for shaping and assembly

2 Cut around the outside of each part of the plane with a craft knife. Do use a new, sharp blade for this operation as a blunt blade will be next to useless when it comes to cutting the more intricate areas of the model.

3 Place the plane wings in position beneath the fuselage as shown. Place the engine nacelles in position. Mark the position of the engine nacelle with a pencil so you know where to begin sanding off the wings.

◄ Check the position of the wing against the fuselage prior to marking out and shaping the wing

▲ Mark out the engine nacelle final shape before carving with the minidrill

to a more gentle curve towards the back of the wing which is called the trailing edge. Remove the bulk of the material with a disc sander in your minidrill but take care as the sander will remove balsa very quickly and you do not want to remove more than is necessary. Finish off with a piece of fine sandpaper to leave a smooth, gently curving finish.

4 Sand off the wing to the shape shown in the template. Note, the underside of the wing remains flat while the top surface is shaped into an aerofoil section. This has a steeper curve on the front of the wing, known as the leading edge, and it tapers away

5 Mark out the curve required on the engine nacelles. These will become a left- and right-handed pair and are not interchangeable. Mark the curve as shown on the template with a soft pencil, taking care not to dig the point of the pencil into the balsa wood which is rather soft. The drum sander will carve out the waste material leaving a realistic curve to the finished parts. Finish off by rubbing the edges with a piece of fine sandpaper until you have achieved a smooth finish.

▶ Round off the fuselage section with the disc sander in the minidrill

6 Glue the wing section and the two engine nacelles carefully into position. Check carefully before you apply the glue that all the parts – fuselage, wing and engine nacelles – line up in their correct positions. You can stick them together with balsa cement if you wish, but PVA woodworking glue is possibly a better adhesive to use. When the glue has set thoroughly, use the disc sander to round off the fuselage section roughly and then sandpaper to a good smooth finish.

7 Fit the air-flow modifiers to the wings in the position shown on the template overleaf. Carve out the insides of these little parts with a parallel burr fitted to your minidrill. Do take extra care with these parts because they are little and will break easily if even a small amount of additional pressure is applied. You will need to angle the inside edge to fit the slope of the wing until you achieve a good tight fit. These little parts will also become a left- and right-handed pair and will not be interchangeable. Then, once you are satisfied with the fit, glue these in place on each side of the wing as shown and leave them to set properly.

8 Shape the tail plane as you did for the wings, and glue it in place on the rear of the fuselage. Allow the glue to set. Carry out any final sanding you may find necessary. Before painting the plane, you can cut a slot in the forward part of the fuselage for catapult launching.

9 Decorate the plane as you wish. Test the plane for balance. You will usually need to add some nose weight to make the plane fly satisfactorily. You will have to discover the amount of weight your own aeroplane needs by experimentation, but as a general guide, a couple of 10mm (⅜in) plain washers cemented into a slot cut into the nose of the aircraft will usually be adequate.

▲ Use a parallel burr in the minidrill to finely carve the inside of the air-flow modifiers

▼ The completed model ready for final decoration

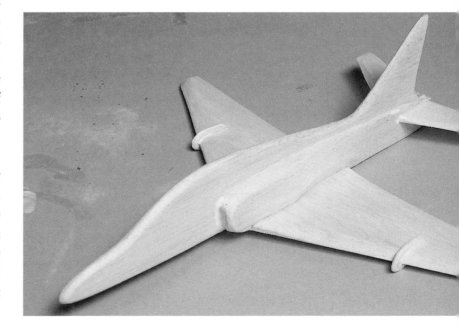

HAWK JET (Red Arrows)
Cutting pattern

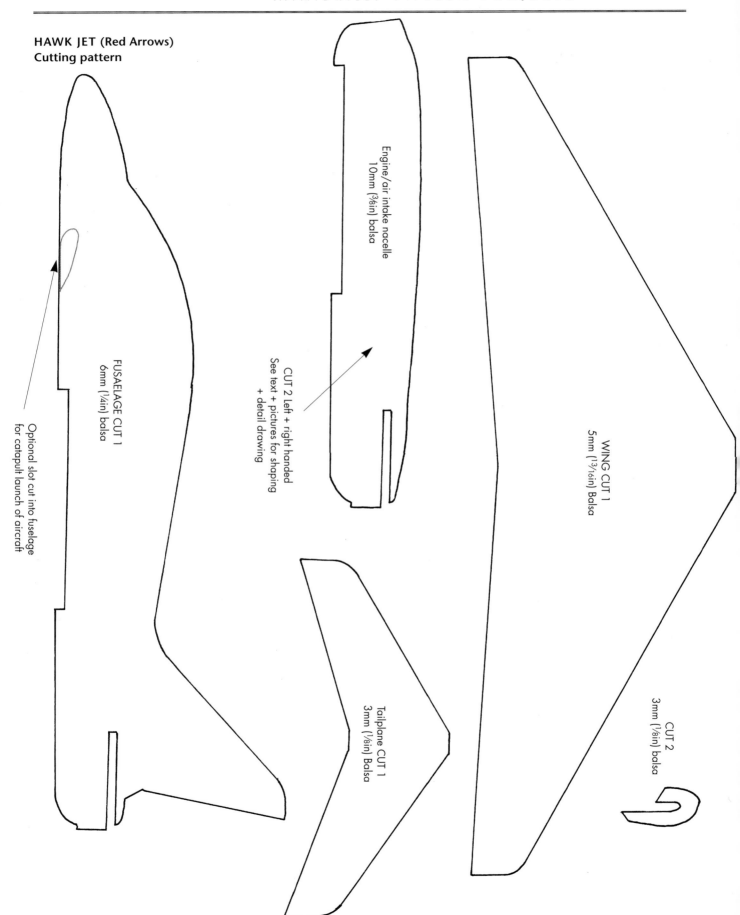

Engine/air intake nacelle
10mm (³⁄₈in) balsa

CUT 2 Left + right handed
See text + pictures for shaping
+ detail drawing

FUSAELAGE CUT 1
6mm (¼in) balsa

Optional slot cut into fuselage
for catapult launch of aircraft

WING CUT 1
5mm (¹³⁄₁₆in) Balsa

CUT 2
3mm (¹⁄₈in) balsa

Tailplane CUT 1
3mm (¹⁄₈in) Balsa

HAWK JET (Red Arrows)
Parts layout

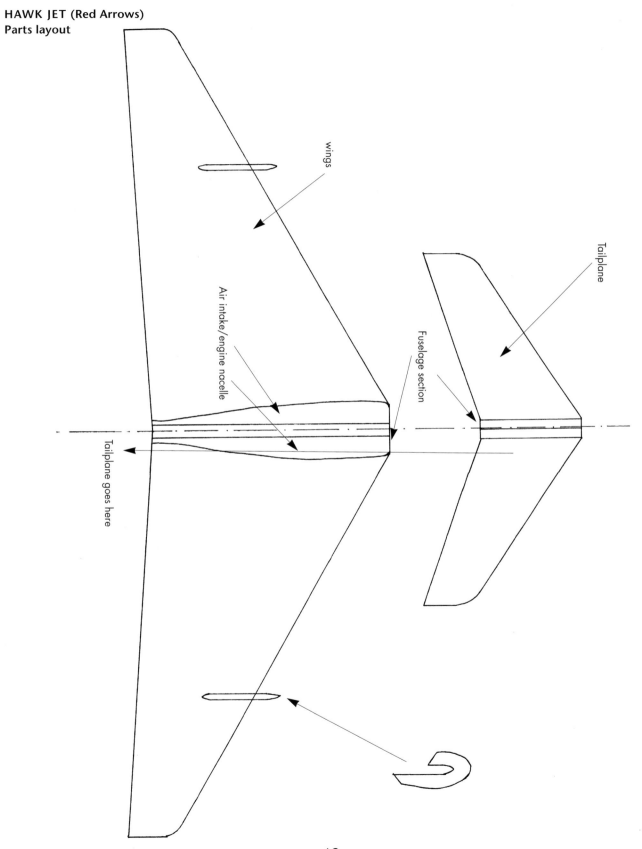

wings

Air intake/engine nacelle

Tailplane

Fuselage section

Tailplane goes here

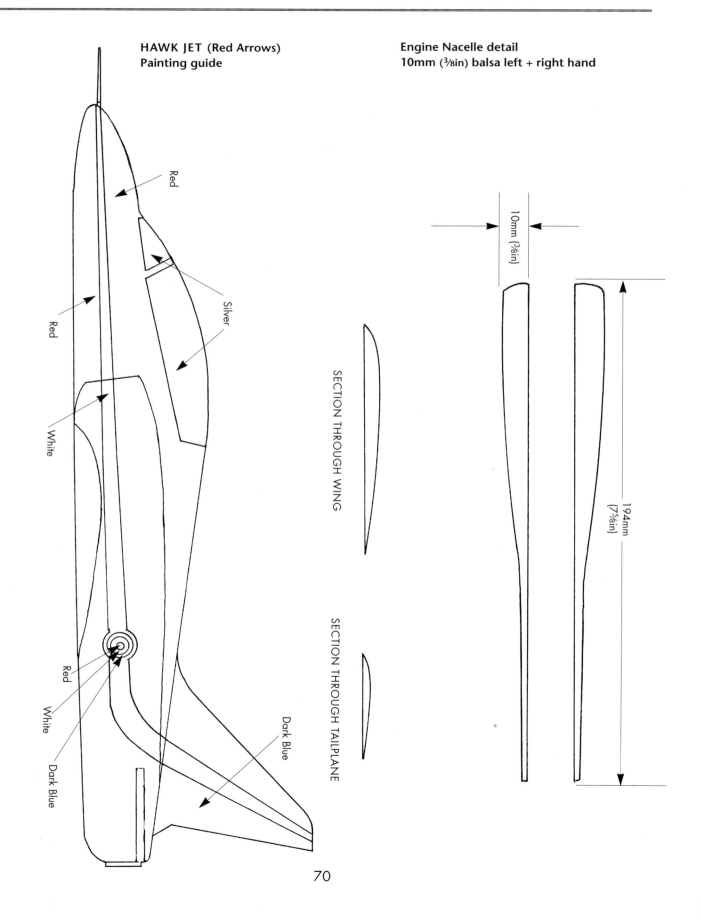

HAWK JET (Red Arrows)
Painting guide

Red

Red

White

Silver

Red

White

Dark Blue

Dark Blue

SECTION THROUGH WING

SECTION THROUGH TAILPLANE

Engine Nacelle detail
10mm (³⁄₈in) balsa left + right hand

10mm (³⁄₈in)

194mm
(7⁵⁄₈in)

70

Cribbage set

There are quite a number of holes to drill for a cribbage board (124 to be precise). They are arranged be in a neat pattern on the top of the board so accurate vertical drilling is required. It will be an advantage to have a drill stand for this task. You can either make one, as described in the minidrill accessories, or you may have a ready-made one.

The set consists of a board, which forms the top panel of the set. This is hinged to the centre section of the box which contains the playing cards, score pad and the pegs used for scoring while the game is in progress. The final part is simply a bottom panel which attaches to the underside of the centre section to complete the box.

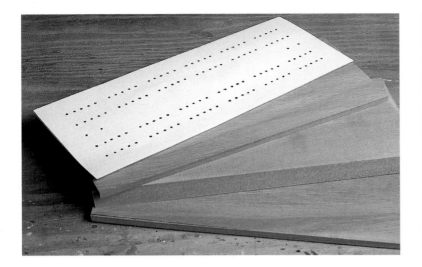

▲ The set of panels and the pattern ready to begin construction

1 Make up a paper pattern from the template. Stick this accurately in place on the top piece of 6mm (¼in) wood. Make sure it is aligned or the hole matrix will not be straight.

2 Take the 20mm (¾in) thick panel, which will form the centre section, and mark out the internal cutout from the template and drill a starter hole for the saw blade to pass through. Use a jigsaw or a fretsaw to make the internal cutout. The example shown here was cut out using a powered fretsaw. Sand the internal edge smooth when the cutout is completed.

► Making the starter hole for the internal cutout on the centre section of the box

◄ Making the pilot holes in the bottom panel for the brass panel pins

▼ The drill stand set up for drilling the hole matrix in the top panel

3 Drill six pilot holes for the fixing pins around the edges of the bottom panel. Mark these out and select a drill bit to make the correct sized pilot hole for the brass panel pins you have. This will be quite small, usually 1mm (1/32in). The joint will be glued as well so further pins will not be needed.

4 Set up the panel in the drill stand and fit a 3.2mm (1/8in) drill bit in the chuck of your minidrill. Carefully line up the centre hole of the bottom row on the pattern. Add a strip of straight timber to act as a rest and clamp it in place on the worktable of the drill stand. Drill the first hole and then slide the panel along to complete the rest of the first row of holes. Drill the rest of the holes for the matrix. Place a piece of scrap wood behind the panel to prevent the wood being broken away from the back of the panel when the drill bit breaks through the back of the wood.

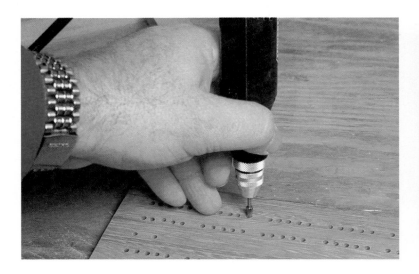

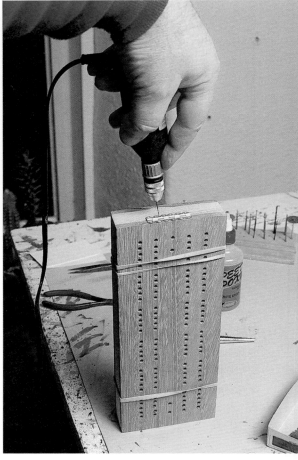

▲ Ream out the holes with a taper burr to make putting in and taking out the pegs easier

▼ The box clamped with a couple of strong elastic bands prior to marking the positions for the hinge and clasp

5 Remove your minidrill from the stand and fit a tapered burr in the chuck. Ream out each of the holes so that they have a taper which widens out towards the top of the board. This will make the pegs easier to insert and remove quickly.

6 Place the hinge in position on the centre section and mark out the fixing pin holes. Add a little dual-epoxy resin underneath the hinge plate and gently tap home the fixing pins.

▲ Use a minidrill to make the pilot holes for the hinge pins

Once the pins have been started in their holes use a nail punch to finish off tapping home each pin to avoid damaging the hinge.

7 Lay the top in position on the centre section of the box and mark the corresponding holes for the lower part of the hinge. Do the same as before. Be careful not to allow the dual-epoxy resin to reach the hinge pin. Fix the lower part of the hinge so that the lid is secure.

8 Attach the top part of the securing clip at the other end of the top panel. Fit this in the same way as you fitted the hinge, taking care not to let the epoxy resin adhesive come into contact with the hinge pin. Once this has been completed, use the top part of the clasp to accurately mark out the position required for the lower part of the clasp. Hold the two pieces together with a couple of strong rubber bands while you mark out the hole positions.

9 Glue and pin the bottom of the box in place and put it aside until all the glue has set completely.

10 Take the four dowel joints and make up the set of pegs for the game. Set up your minidrill in its stand and fit the sanding disc into the chuck. Hold onto one end of each dowel joint and rotate it against the sanding disc so that all but the top 10mm (⅜in) of each peg is reduced to a gentle taper which fits well into the hole matrix in the top panel. Check each peg as you turn it down so that you don't reduce the shank of each peg by too much.

11 Colour the tops of one pair of the pegs you have made so that one pair is easily and quickly distinguishable from the other pair. Decorate the cribbage set to your own preference. The example shown here was simply wax polished and buffed to a gentle shine with a soft cloth.

▶ The set of pegs needed for the game

▲ Buff the completed box with wax polish and a soft duster

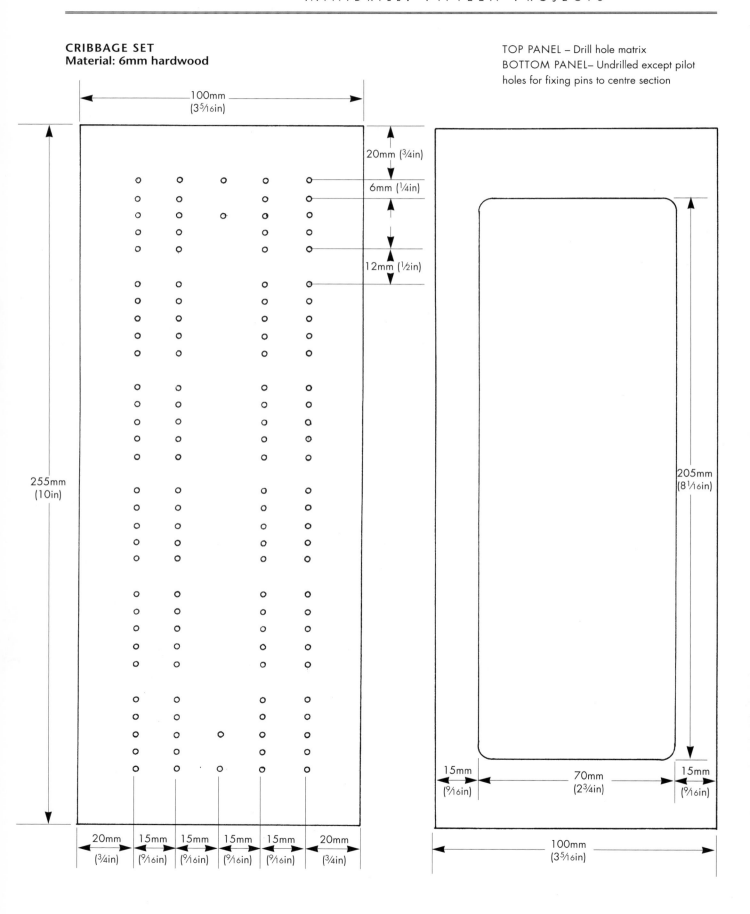

CRIBBAGE SET
Material: 6mm hardwood

TOP PANEL – Drill hole matrix
BOTTOM PANEL– Undrilled except pilot
holes for fixing pins to centre section

100mm
(3⁵⁄₁₆in)

20mm (¾in)

6mm (¼in)

12mm (½in)

255mm
(10in)

205mm
(8¹⁄₁₆in)

20mm
(¾in)

15mm
(⁹⁄₁₆in)

15mm
(⁹⁄₁₆in)

15mm
(⁹⁄₁₆in)

15mm
(⁹⁄₁₆in)

20mm
(¾in)

15mm
(⁹⁄₁₆in)

70mm
(2¾in)

15mm
(⁹⁄₁₆in)

100mm
(3⁵⁄₁₆in)

Puppet

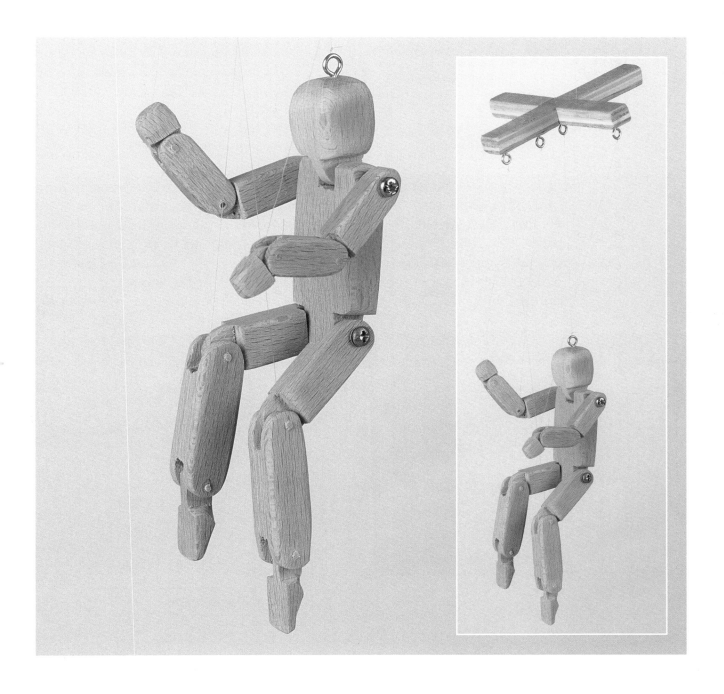

YOU WILL NEED:

Small pieces of hardwood of any type (the dimensions of each piece are given on the template)

Four flat washers of a diameter to suit the screws

About three wooden cocktail sticks, to make the joints of the puppet

Roundhead woodscrews

A little fishing line or thread

Six miniature screw eyes

▼The pre-cut wooden blanks which form the various parts of the puppet

This project details a small-scale puppet which can be made with the minidrill. The horizontal drill stand (see page 17) will prove useful for rounding off and shaping individual parts of the puppet. The threads of the puppet are suspended from a crosspiece, much the same as a traditional puppet. The joint pins are made from small lengths cut from wooden cocktail sticks and the main body parts are made from small scraps of hardwood. Beech was used in the example shown here, but almost any available pieces of hardwood will do just as well.

Although this particular puppet is basically humanoid in form, the same technique could be applied to any animal or bird. The features of the head have been deliberately left blank so you can use your own ideas for making up the features.

1 Cut out all the main component parts of the puppet using the detailed dimensions given on the template. This can be done with a variety of different tools. A coping saw will suffice for the body parts of the puppet as they are quite small and intricate.

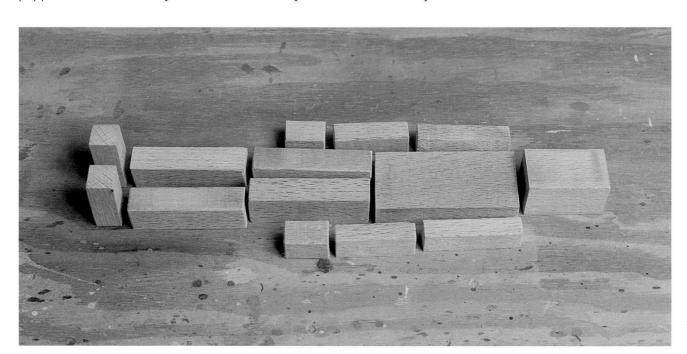

◀ Shape the joints using the sander attachment in the minidrill

2 Begin making the internal cutouts for the lower leg and lower arm pieces. Drill a hole at the inner end of the joint the same diameter as the slot and then cut down to the hole with your coping saw. Do not square off the roundness left by the drilled holes. Mark up the other half of the joint and saw it out with a coping saw.

3 Drill a small hole right through the socket parts of the joints. Use a drill bit that is fractionally smaller than the diameter of the wooden cocktail sticks. Make sure the hole is drilled straight so that there will be no distortion when the joint is assembled. Make another hole in the centre part of the joints. This hole should be drilled out with a larger drill bit so that it is a clearance hole for the wooden cocktail

stick. This will allow the joint to rotate freely about the centre part of the wooden pin. Make sure that you repeat this process for all of the joints.

▼ A joint marked up ready for cutting out

▲ Use the coping saw to cut out the joint

▲ Drill through the joint so that a cocktail stick will fit snugly through it

► The complete limb ready for assembly with the cocktail stick joint pins

6 Fit your minidrill to the horizontal drill stand and use sanding discs to round off the arms and legs to achieve a smoother finish which is less square and more convincing. This will probably not matter too much if you plan to clothe your puppet once it is finished although hard edges can show through fine material so it is best to round things off at this stage. The hands and feet should be trimmed down by quite a bit from the original block of wood from which they were made so that they resemble the real thing a little more closely. Round off the head and body in the same way as the hands and feet.

4 Cut away the part of the top of the upper legs parts where they will join on to the body. There are cut-away portions to allow the leg to hang directly below the body section.

▲ Thread the joint pin, a cocktail stick, through the joint and cut it to length

5 Assemble the arms and legs. Place the inner part of each joint in position inside the other half of the joint and push a wooden cocktail stick into the outer part of the joint. Tap it lightly with a mallet so that it passes through the inner part of the joint and then out from the other side of the outer part of the joint. Next cut the pointed ends of the cocktail sticks off using a cutting disc fitted into your minidrill, or a pair of end cutters. Sand down the remaining part of the cocktail stick so that it is flush with the surface of the leg or arm joint. No glue is required.

▶ Attach the legs of the puppet to the torso using screws and plain washers

7 Drill clearance holes through each upper leg joint where it will join onto the torso to suit the screws you intend to use. Do make sure that your selected screws will not reach beyond halfway across the torso, otherwise the two screws will meet and you will not be able to tighten them sufficiently.

81

▲ The completed puppet ready for attaching the strings

▲ Make the crosspiece from two strips of wood half jointed and glued together

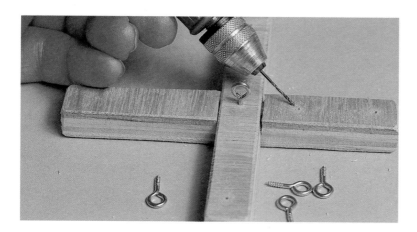

Pass the screws through the leg joints and add on a couple of plain washers over the screw so that the leg is spaced away from the body a little. Drill a pilot hole into either side of the body in the correct position. Screw the legs into the body. Do the screw up until it is just tight enough to prevent the leg from moving and then slacken off a little so that the leg is free to move on its joint.

8 Attach the arms in a similar way. You need to attach one arm with a much longer screw so that it passes through the arm, the torso and the head, and a little way into the far side of torso. One screw provides the pivot for both the arm and the head. Drill a clearance hole for the screw up to the head then drill a pilot hole for the part of the screw thread that will actually secure the whole joint. Fit the arm and the head onto the torso. Add on a couple of plain washers between the arm and torso to act as spacers so that the lower part of the arm and the hand swing clear of the leg. The remaining arm is attached with a shorter screw. Select one that almost reaches where the longer screw finishes. The arm is now attached with another pair of plain washers and if the screw is just a little too long, you can cut off a small part of it with a cutting disc fitted into your minidrill.

◄ Use the minidrill with a very small drill bit to make the pilot holes for the miniature screw eyes that will attach the strings

9 Make the crosspiece from two short strips of wood or ply. Cut a notch out of the centre of each to make a cross-halved joint and glue the pieces together, clamping until they are dry. Both pieces should sit flush with each other. Then, drill pilot holes for the miniature screw eyes so they do not split the wood when you screw them into place. Once you have screwed them into place as shown, drill tiny holes to thread the strings through on the puppet. These tiny holes are drilled into the upper parts of the joints where the knees and elbows would be. Carefully thread the string through these holes, checking the length, and attach the strings to the crosspiece that will support the puppet. Decorate and/or dress your puppet in whatever fashion you think best.

◄ Use the same tiny drill bit to make the attachment holes for the threads that connect the limbs of the puppet to the crosspiece

◄ Thread up the joints with string and attach them to the crosspiece

MINI PUPPET
Material: hardwood

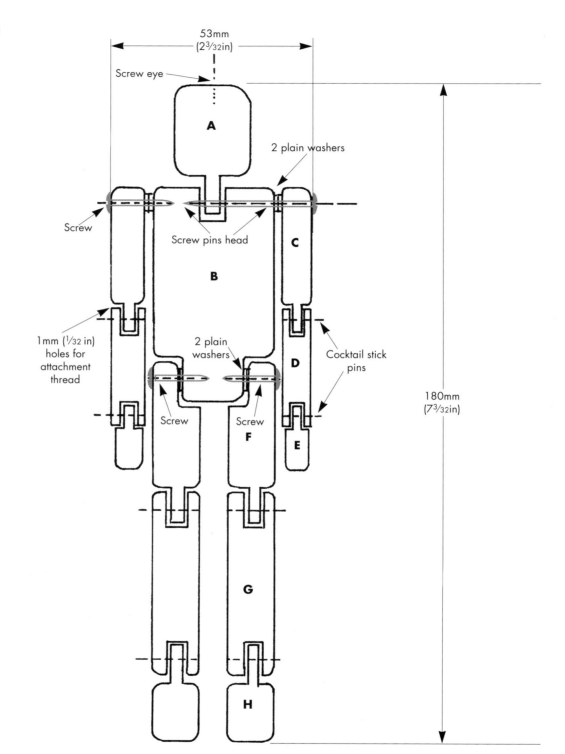

53mm
(2³/₃₂in)

Screw eye

2 plain washers

A

Screw

Screw pins head

C

B

1mm (¹/₃₂ in)
holes for
attachment
thread

2 plain
washers

Cocktail stick
pins

D

Screw

Screw

F

E

180mm
(7³/₃₂in)

DIMENSIONS

A – 35 x 20 x 20mm
(1³/₈ x ³/₄ x ³/₄in)

B – 59 x 32 x 12mm
(1³/₈ x ³/₄ x ³/₄in)

C – 40 x 10 x 12mm
(1⁹/₁₆ x ³/₈ x ¹/₂in)

D – 32 x 10 x 12mm
(1¹/₄ x ³/₈ x ¹/₂in)

E – 20 x 6 x 12mm
(³/₄ x ¹/₄ x ¹/₂in)

F – 45 x 12 x 12mm
(1³/₄ x ¹/₂ x ¹/₂in)

G – 50 x 12 x 12mm
(2 x ¹/₂ x ¹/₂in)

H – 25 x 12 x 12mm
(1 x ¹/₂ x ¹/₂in)

G

H

Miniature projects

Love spoon

This little project is a smaller version of the more usual-size Welsh love spoon. For the example shown here, an offcut from a salvaged piece of mahogany was used from an old Georgian dresser that was beyond economic repair. Different types of hardwood can be used equally well to make up this attractive little original design of Celtic love spoon.

The rope parts of the spoon design intertwine, passing over and under each other. In the language of the original love spoon, this symbolizes that the two lovers will be eternally enmeshed because the design has no beginning or end.

1 Make up a paper pattern from the template. Clean up the piece of hardwood with sandpaper, particularly on the top and bottom faces of the piece of wood. Stick the cutting pattern in place so that the design runs along the grain of the wood. This will give you maximum strength in the finished love spoon.

2 Make starter holes through the wood where there are gaps in the design. These gaps are between coils of the rope and in the heart cutout at the top of the spoon. This will give you a starting point to begin your carving.

3 Fit a burr in your minidrill and cut down each side of the rope strands, referring to the template. If you have one, use a burr which roughly resembles a part of an inverted cone. When you have made an initial cut down each strand passing below its neighbour, start to round off all the strands on the design with a ball-shaped burr. Clean up with some fine sandpaper afterwards in any case.

▼ Drilling the starter holes before starting the carving operation

TIP

The use of a cutting pattern is essential for an intricate design of this nature and will allow you to make accurate starter cuts on the design which will make the completed love spoon follow the original design accurately. Attach the cutting pattern to the wood with a little spray mount adhesive.

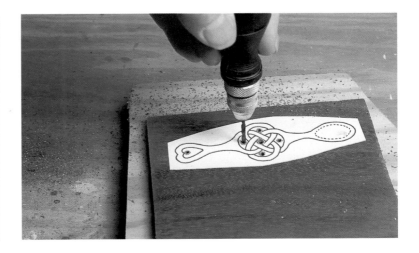

► Carve out the bowl of the spoon using the dotted line on the cutting pattern as a guide

4 Keep the ball-shaped burr in your minidrill and carve out the waste material from the bowl of the spoon. Make a good smooth job and carve out enough wood to make a reasonably deep recess in the bowl. The dotted line on the cutting pattern shows the extent to which the hollowing out operation should be done.

5 Round off the stem of the spoon, working your way up to the heart-shaped top. The inner shape of the heart on top of the spoon is too tight for the round burr and you will need to change to a very small taper burr to complete the shape.

▲ Carry out the final carving on the internal parts of the design with a fine burr

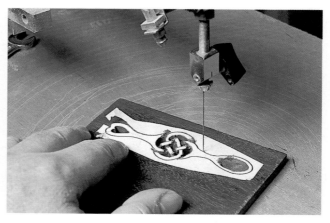

▲ Cut the spoon shape from the waste wood

6 Using a padsaw or a scrollsaw, cut around the outline of the spoon, removing it from the surrounding waste material.

7 Turn the spoon over and remove the bulk of the waste material with a straight burr, taking care to follow the line of the curve on the inside of the spoon's bowl. Cut away a little material at a time and check the shape of the bowl of the spoon. Complete the carving with a strip of fine sandpaper to smooth over all the edges of the design front and back so that the finished object is visually attractive.

8 Decorate the spoon with a coat of varnish with a stain. The originals tend to have a dark finish and for authenticity, it might be a good idea to follow the practice. The ideal range of colours goes from a deep mahogany to a Jacobean oak which is a very dark brown indeed.

▲ Use a round burr to shape the reverse of the spoon

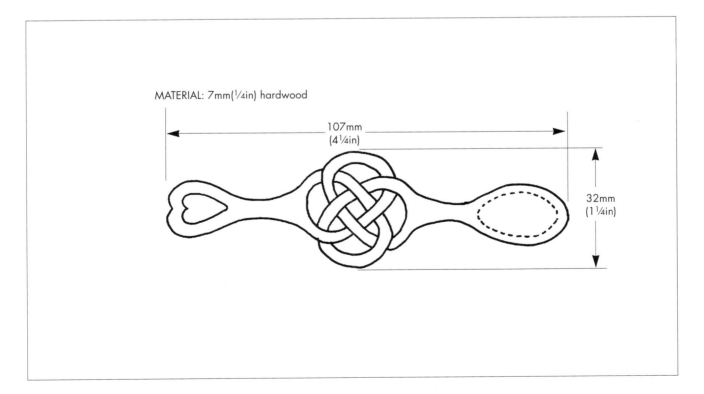

MATERIAL: 7mm(¼in) hardwood

107mm
(4¼in)

32mm
(1¼in)

Tree

YOU WILL NEED:

A few clippings from a hedge, shrub or small tree

A small scrap of 9mm (³⁄₈in) MDF or hardwood for the base

A few wooden cocktail sticks to act as miniature dowel joints

Wood glue and dual-epoxy resin

A couple of small bits of gravel in interesting shapes

Cotton wool balls

A length of florist's wire (usually covered in green plastic)

A tub of dried mixed herbs

Acrylic paint, such as green or brown

Satin or matt varnish

▲ A selection of clippings suitable for making up a scale model tree

This project is an ideal application for the basic minidrill kit. By following the techniques shown, you will be able to produce realistic scale model trees. Most of the ingredients can be gleaned from the garden and around the house.

1 Select the main trunk for the tree from the clippings you have taken. Choose the angle you want the tree to sit at on the MDF base and mark the correct slant on the trunk. Cut to the angle you want with a cutting disc in the chuck of your minidrill, or use a coping saw if you prefer. Be careful to make the cut flat so that it will sit properly on the base.

2 Mark out an interesting shape for the base of the tree on the scrap of MDF. This can, of course, be any shape you like, but it will look best if it fits appropriately into the scale landscape in which you intend using it. Cut it out to the shape.

▲ Drill a hole in the base and the bottom of the tree to accommodate the dowel rods

▲ Fit a length of wooden cocktail stick in place in the base of the trunk of the tree

3 Mark the position on the base where you want to mount the tree. Select a drill bit which will give a reasonably tight fit for the wooden cocktail sticks. Drill vertically down into the base to make an anchor point for the cocktail stick dowel. Carefully drill a corresponding hole into the tree trunk. Cut off the sharpened point of a cocktail stick and glue the blunted cocktail stick into the trunk of the tree. Measure the length you will need to fit into the hole in the base and cut the cocktail stick off to length. Glue this in place with wood glue and leave aside to dry completely.

4 Fit a drum sander in the chuck of your minidrill and roughly shape the edges of the base so that there are no unnatural right angles left. Use a round burr to cut away and rough up the rest of the base to give it a much more natural look. Hollow out a couple of areas to fit the gravel which can represent scale rocks with your burr.

► Use a drum sander in the minidrill to roughly shape the edges of the base

◄ Hollow out scoops in the base using a round burr to hold the gravel

5 Select some suitable branches to add to the main trunk. These are cut off from the remaining cuttings you have. Make the cuts at a suitable angle so that they look natural. Drill holes into the ends of each of the branches with the drill bit used earlier for the wooden cocktail sticks. Glue bits of cocktail stick in place to act as dowel joints. Mark where each branch will go on the tree and the length of cocktail stick needed to reach almost through the trunk. Cut the dowel sticks to length. Drill corresponding holes into the trunk at the correct angle. Glue the branches into place. Leave the glue to set completely.

6 Add some more wood glue in a ring around the base of the tree so that it forms a raised area which can be machined with a suitable burr in your minidrill to resemble the root system of the tree.

7 The smallest branches are made from short lengths of the florist's wire. Select a drill bit that will enable you to drill holes that are a reasonably tight fit for the diameter of the wire. Choose points on the upper branches

▼ Mark where the branch will attach to the trunk, checking the length of cocktail stick dowel

▲ Drill right through the upper branches of the tree so the length of florist's wire can be threaded through the holes

8 Paint the base and the tree itself. Colour the base grass green and give the trunk and branches of the tree itself a coat of brown. Make up the acrylic paint mix for the foliage. Mix the acrylic paint with some water and dip the cotton wool balls into the mix so they take up enough of the paint to colour them, but do not let them soak completely, otherwise they will take a long time to dry. When you have coloured all the cotton balls, put them aside on a piece of kitchen paper to dry out thoroughly.

and drill holes right through the branches in those positions. Thread short lengths of the wire through these holes and secure them in place with a little dab of dual-epoxy resin. Once the wires are secure in their positions, bend them into more realistic shapes.

9 Thread the cotton wool balls onto the wires and onto other parts of the tree where they will look appropriate. If you need to place the cotton wool in parts where there is no wire or other protrusion to hold them in place, use a dab of glue to secure them.

10 Give each cotton wool blob a generous coat of varnish, applying it gently with a soft brush and then sprinkling the chopped dried herbs over the cotton wool so that a good covering of the herbs sticks to the cotton wool and its varnish. Don't be concerned if there are any odd bare patches as you can go over the tree again later and finish off any little areas that are in need of more attention. It makes sense to stand the tree on its base inside a tray so that the surplus dried herbs drop off into the tray for re-use.

◄ Trim the wire to length before securing it in place with glue

◄ Coat the cotton
wool balls with
paint mix and
leave to dry
thoroughly

11 When the varnish used to attach
your foliage to the tree has had a
chance to dry thoroughly, give the
whole tree a further coat of satin or
matt varnish. This will give an
authentic sheen to the leaves and bark
of the tree and is probably best applied
from an aerosol spray of varnish if you
have one available. If not, apply the
varnish very gently with a soft brush,
taking care not to dislodge your leaves.
Glue the gravel in place with dual-
epoxy resin adhesive.

▲ Coat the tree
with varnish and
cover with dried
mixed herbs

TIP
It is a good idea to secure
cotton wool balls in place with
some adhesive, particularly if the
finished tree is going to be handled.

Long case clock

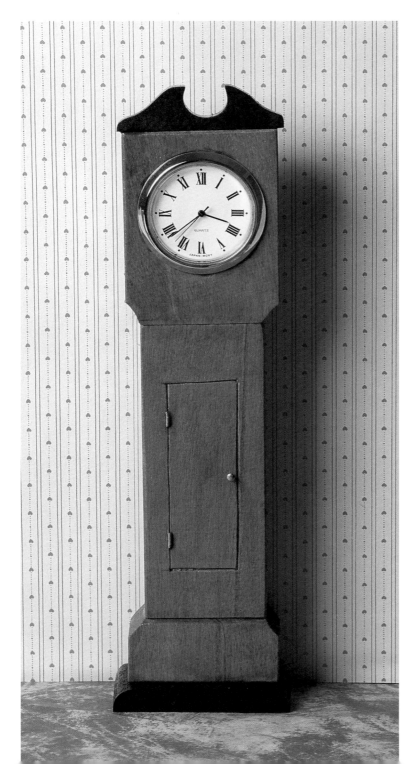

This little project has been designed in ¹⁄12th scale so it can not only be used on its own as a decorative clock about the house, but will also find a place in any period dolls' house. Although this project could be carved from one piece of wood, this design is assembled from several parts, allowing for the use of much smaller scraps of hardwood. The actual clock movement is a ready-made quartz watch which is widely available at a nominal cost. The clock insert used here has a neoprene ring around its outer case with little projections to allow it to be a simple but secure push fit into the case.

Providing you are careful when marking out and measuring, this is a simple project. The individual parts of the clock case are jointed using cut off pieces of wooden cocktail sticks to act as miniature dowel joints, making the whole assembly mechanically strong enough to withstand handling. This is important if children are to use the clock in a dolls' house.

◄ Clean up the surfaces of the pieces with a drum sander prior to assembly

1 Make up a full-size paper pattern of the parts of the clock using the template. Then, use the paper pattern to cut out the basic shapes from the hardwood offcuts. These can be cut with virtually any saw in the usual way.

YOU WILL NEED:

A few small offcuts of hardwood

A couple of wooden cocktail sticks

Wood glue and dual-epoxy resin

A quartz clock insert

One small brass panel pin to make the door knob and hinges

Varnish to decorate

Just cut them out as plain blocks and use the minidrill fitted with a drum sander to clean their surfaces. Lay out the five pieces which make up the clock on the paper pattern to check that all the pieces have been cut accurately.

2 A horizontal drill stand would be useful at this point, see page 17 for details of how to make one of these. Fit the minidrill in the drill stand and fit a drum sander. Refer to the template for the actual shapes required for each piece. Gently run the pieces along the drum sander until they match the template. Check each piece against each other as they go to ensure that they fit. Only a light touch against the sanding drum will be necessary for accurate shaping.

4 Hollow out the recess for the clock movement. Measure your clock carefully and adjust the pattern accordingly. Stick the appropriate part of the cutting pattern in place on the wooden blank with a little spray mount adhesive. Use a ball-shaped burr to hollow out the recess to the required depth. Use an inverted-cone burr to cut away the remaining wood until you reach the marked line you need all over the recess. Check the recess with the clock insert when you are almost finished. The fit should be snug, so don't cut too much material out of the recess. Remove the remains of the cutting pattern and clean up the recess with sandpaper.

▲ Use the minidrill with a burr fitted to carve out the recess for the clock insert

3 To shape the top piece of the clock, cut out the pattern shape and stick it in place on your wood blank with a little spray mount adhesive. Fit a straight burr into the chuck of your minidrill and gently carve away the waste wood until you reach the cutting line on the pattern. Finish off by smoothing the piece with fine sandpaper.

▼ Check the fit of the clock insert

5 When all the pieces have been shaped and matched to each other for fit, go over all the pieces with a strip of very fine sandpaper. Mark out the positions in each clock piece for the peg joints. The precise location of each pair of peg holes is not very important as long as the holes line up precisely with the neighbouring pieces so that there is no distortion or twisting when you come to assemble them later on. Drill the holes to take the cocktail stick dowel rods.

TIP

Make absolutely sure the peg holes are in alignment before drilling. Make up a paper pattern to locate the holes if you are unsure of the accuracy of the hole placing.

► Use the horizontal drill stand to hold the minidrill while shaping the clock parts

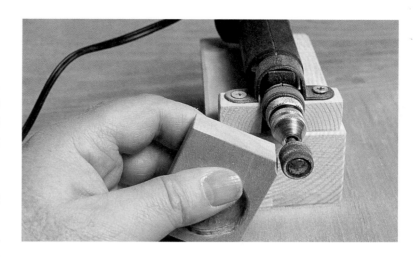

6 Cut the cocktail sticks to length. Apply a little wood glue to the dowel joint and assemble all the parts together. Then leave the adhesive to set completely.

7 The door of the clock is false. Mark out the door with a pencil line, then cut along each side of the pencil line with a small, sharp craft knife creating a V-shaped groove around the edges of the door. Cut the hinges from a couple of brass pins so you have two pieces of brass pin about 3–4mm (⅛in–5⁄32in) in length. Glue these in place with dual-epoxy resin. Drill a pilot hole as shown on the template and tap in another brass pin to represent the door handle. Complete the decoration with whatever varnish or combination of stain and varnish you wish to use.

▲ Use a craft knife to cut a V-shaped groove around the door shape

◄ Mix a little dual-epoxy resin adhesive to secure the hinges, cut from brass pins, in position

8 When the varnish has dried completely, all that remains to do is to set the correct time on your clock insert. Then, fit it into its place in the recess at the top of the clock.

▶ Drill a pilot hole for the brass pin which will form the handle of the clock case door

▲ Inserting the clock movement into the completed clock case

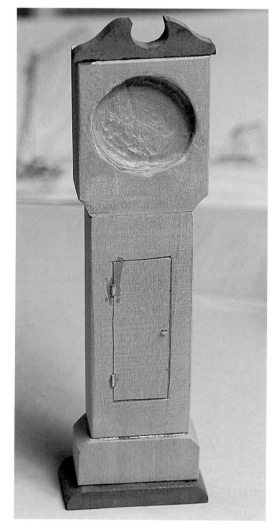

◀ The completed case ready for decoration

CLOCK ASSEMBLY PLAN

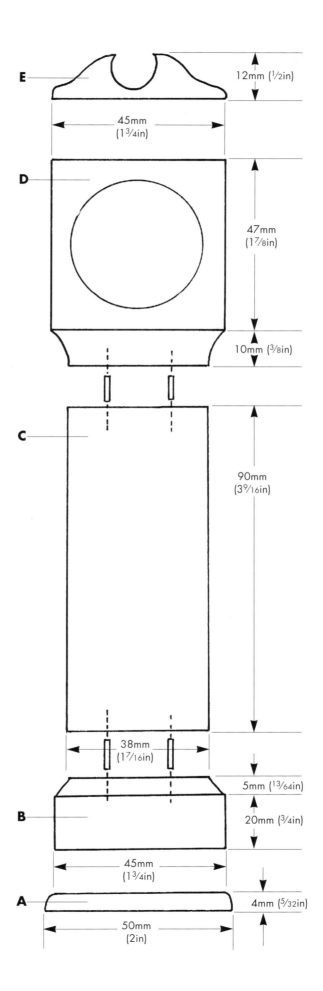

E

12mm (1/2in)

45mm
(1 3/4in)

D

47mm
(1 7/8in)

10mm (3/8in)

C

90mm
(3 9/16in)

38mm
(1 7/16in)

5mm (1 3/64in)

B

20mm (3/4in)

45mm
(1 3/4in)

A

4mm (5/32in)

50mm
(2in)

CLOCK DETAIL PLAN

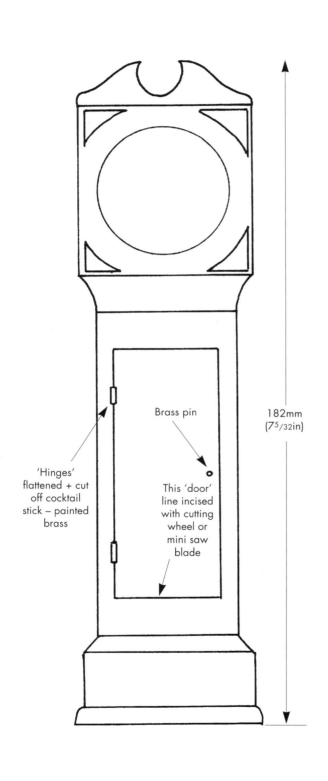

'Hinges'
flattened + cut
off cocktail
stick – painted
brass

Brass pin

This 'door'
line incised
with cutting
wheel or
mini saw
blade

182mm
(7⁵/₃₂in)

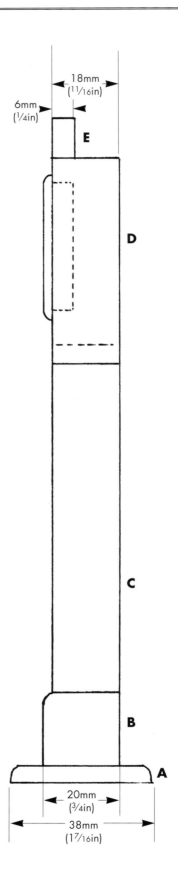

18mm
(1¹/₁₆in)

6mm
(¹/₄in)

E

D

C

B

A

20mm
(³/₄in)

38mm
(1⁷/₁₆in)

Decorative projects

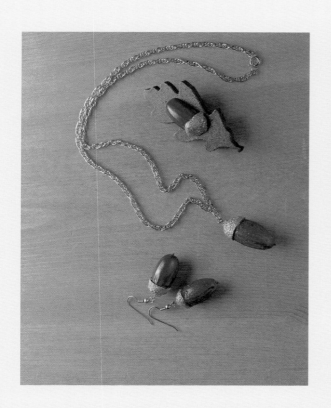

Intarsia panel

YOU WILL NEED:

A piece of hardwood of around 6–10mm (¼in–⅜in) thick and 184mm x 162.5mm (7¼in x 6⅜in)

A thin sheet of ply or backing card, of the same size as the picture panel to make a backing sheet

A frame

Paints and varnishes to decorate

Dual-epoxy resin (ordinary PVA or other wood glues will also work as well but take longer to set properly)

A sheet of either glass or polythene to lay out the glued pieces for reassembly

Miniature drum sander with medium and fine sandpaper drums for use in your minidrill

An intarsia panel is designed rather like a jigsaw. It is made from a picture drawn onto a sheet of wood or other material, cut out into its individual pieces or picture elements which are then rounded off and shaped, painted or decorated and then ressembled as a complete picture on a backing board.

This project uses a saw (I used a scrollsaw) and a minidrill. You will find the lathe accessory, without its tool rest, described on page 24, will come in useful when shaping the pieces of the panel, but you can also manage without one.

1 Make sure the surface of the panel of wood is perfectly flat and has a good smooth finish. If work is necessary on the panel, sand it carefully with a medium paper to get a reasonable surface and then finish off with a fine or very fine sandpaper to get the best finish you can. Always use the sandpaper on a sanding block to retain the flatness of the surface of the wood.

2 Make up two identical paper patterns. If you are using a picture of your own rather than following the example given here, make sure the picture does not have very small parts. Make sure the picture has lines which reach out to the edge of the frame so that you will be able to cut away all the edge of the panel.

▼ The minidrill clamped to the work bench and fitted with a miniature drum sander ready to shape the panel parts

► Using the drum sander lightly to round off the edges of each of the picture pieces before reassembling on the paper pattern

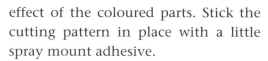

▼ Lightly finishing each piece with very fine sandpaper around the shaped parts

3 Lay the paper pattern in place on the wooden panel. Check that the grain of the wood is used to its best advantage so that some of the wood can be left natural, enhancing the

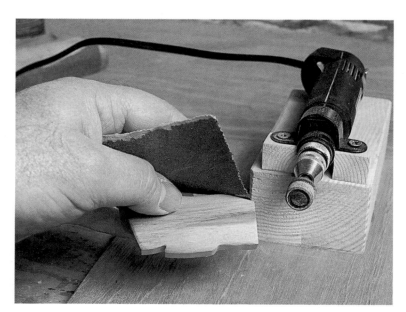

effect of the coloured parts. Stick the cutting pattern in place with a little spray mount adhesive.

4 Cut the picture pieces out with a hand saw or a power-operated machine, depending on what you have available. The power machine is the better option as it cuts vertically, which is almost essential for this type of project. If you are using a hand saw take great care to make the cuts vertical as you progress through the panel. A fine blade around no. 5 or no. 3 is good for this type of work.

5 Fit your minidrill with either the miniature drum sander or flat disc sander. Shape and round off the pieces of the picture. Finish any rough edges with sandpaper.

The drill will be rotating at high speed so it will remove material very quickly, but if you hold the workpiece too loosely, it could easily snatch and throw the part quite some distance. Practise first on some small scrap pieces of similar wood you may have available until you feel more confident.

6 Decorate all of the pieces before putting the panel back together. Do not paint or varnish any further down the sides of each piece than where your shaping finished. The sides of each piece should be left as bare wood which can take glue easily when the pieces are joined together. Any layers of paint will force the finished pieces apart, leaving an unsightly gap between the pieces when the picture is assembled.

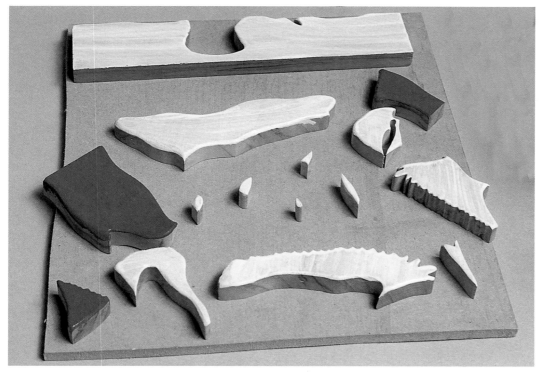

▲ The panel reassembled on the paper pattern showing the rounded-off and shaped individual picture elements

◄ Undercoat the top and rounded-off surfaces of all the pieces

7 Once the paint and varnish has dried thoroughly, reassemble the panel, gluing the pieces to each other on the glass or polythene panel. Some small amounts of the glue will seep through between the individual parts onto the glass or polythene. Once the glue has set properly peel away the polythene or glass sheet and discard it.

8 All that remains now is to complete the project with a suitable frame or other method of display. The kingfisher panel shown here was placed in a plain pine frame with a slightly deeper recess than normal to accommodate the extra thickness of the wooden panel used. The plain pine was decorated with a gold metallic varnish.

► Reassemble the decorated panel using the paper pattern as a guide

INTARSIA PANEL DESIGN

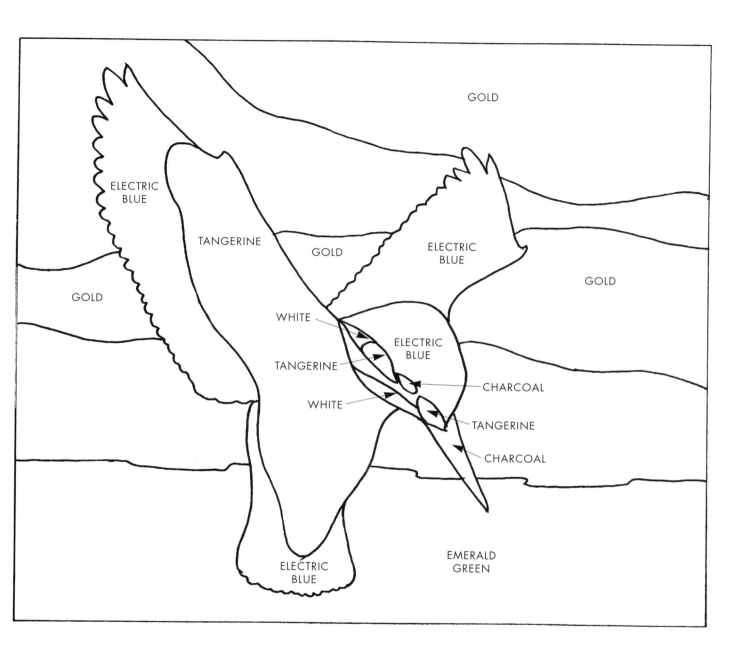

Printing blocks

The minidrill is the perfect tool for making printing blocks in a variety of quite complex shapes. There is a design given here for you to try out, but feel free to use your own ideas if you wish. The template is a double design for using as a mirror image so that left- and right-handed versions are provided, allowing you to maximize the layout potential of the block. A 6mm (¼in) thick piece of MDF makes up the body of the block, with a backing board of made from acrylic sheeting so you can see where the block will be placed.

YOU WILL NEED:

Pieces of MDF of around 6mm (¼in) in thickness to suit the pattern you choose to make

Pieces of acrylic sheet in either 2 or 4mm (¹⁄₁₆ or ⁵⁄₃₂in) thickness to make the backing pieces for the painting blocks

Short pieces of wood around 25mm (1in) square to make the handles

Dual-epoxy resin

▼ The paper template ready to be stuck down onto the MDF blanks with spray mount adhesive

1 Prepare a set of full-size templates of the designs you want to create. Cut out appropriately sized pieces of MDF and stick the paper pattern down onto pieces of MDF using a little spray mount adhesive.

2 Fit your minidrill with an inverted cone-shaped burr and cut along the lines of the pattern, making sure you are cutting on the waste side of the line. Begin to remove the waste material of the background. Make sure that the chuck of the drill, which is rotating at high speed, does not foul the paper pattern. You can avoid this problem by keeping the body of the drill at a reasonable angle to the workpiece and keeping an eye on the drill itself as well as on the cutting line.

3 Once you have cut the outline of each part of the pattern, remove the remains of the paper template. Remove the rest of the waste material between the lines and between the edge of the pattern and the outside edge of the MDF, so that only the painting lines remain. The round burr, the one shaped like a ball, will leave a good smooth finish to the parts of the printing block which are not required to hold paint.

▲ Use the inverted cone burr to cut down along the pattern lines

► Use the ball-shaped burr to remove the remaining waste material from the background of the printing block

112

4 When all the waste material has been removed rub over the whole printing block gently with a piece of fine sandpaper to remove any rough edges. This will leave everything neat and ready to accept paint.

5 Cut out the printing block from the surrounding waste material. Leave a gap of around 3mm (⅛in) between the outer line of the block and the edge of the MDF. You can use a burr for this operation if you like, although the example shown here was actually cut out on a scrollsaw.

▲ Sand over the painting lines gently with fine sandpaper to remove any rough edges

◄ Use a scrollsaw to cut away the printing block from the waste material

6 Measure and mark out the acrylic sheet to make the backing sheets for the printing blocks. Score both sides of the sheet along the cutting line with a craft knife and steel ruler and snap off the pieces. Remove any sharp edges on the acrylic sheet with the help of some fine sandpaper.

► Measure up the acrylic backing sheet using the printing block as a guide

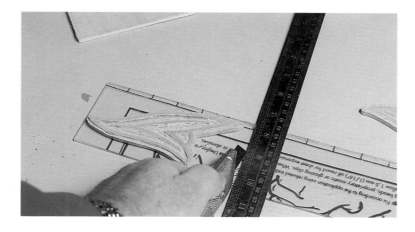

▶ Glue the printing block to the acrylic backing sheet

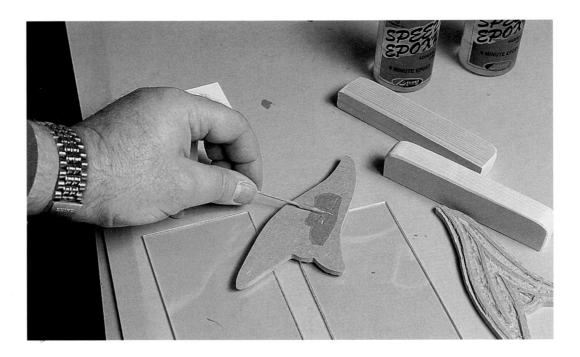

7 Glue the printing block to the acrylic backing sheet with dual-epoxy resin. When the adhesive has set completely, add the simple handles. The handles are made from lengths of 25mm (1in) square soft wood rounded off to form a comfortable grip. It may be worth treating the MDF printing surface with a sealant before you begin using it, as MDF is fairly absorbent.

▶ Bond the soft wood handles to the back of the acrylic backing sheet

PAINTING BLOCKS

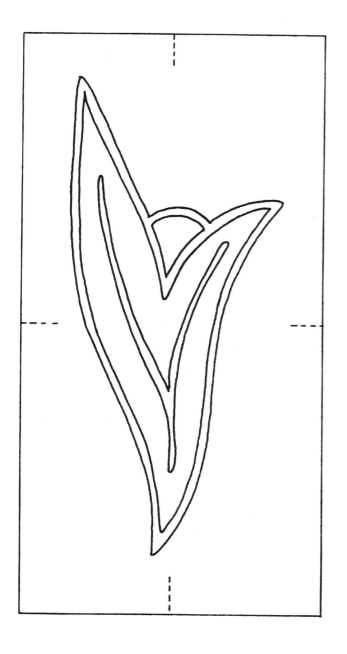
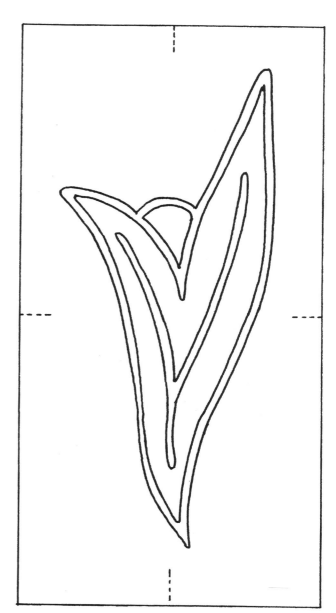

Casket

◄ Stick the pattern in place on the lid of the box

This adaptable little box can be used for jewellery, knick-knacks or just about anything you can think of. This item will be much easier to construct properly if you have built the drill stand outlined earlier in this book or if you have a ready-made drill stand, because the assembly of the panels requires precise drilling. The holes for the brass pins need to be vertical and accurately placed so that the brass pins do not wander off line and puncture the sides of any of the panels.

1 Make a set of patterns using the dimensions given here. Transfer the motif and nail hole positions.

2 Cut out the panels to size accurately. Sand them all smooth, starting with medium sandpaper and completing the job with fine sandpaper. Check the panels against each other to ensure that they will fit properly and the edges all match up.

3 Select the lid panel and position and stick the appropriate pattern in place with a little spray mount. Fit a strip of wood in place on the drilling table of the drill stand and clamp it in place so that you can rest the edge of the lid panel on it when drilling. Check that the panel will be in exactly the right position by sliding your minidrill

YOU WILL NEED:

Pair of miniature brass hinges

Pair of brass clasps

Brass pins for assembling the box

Wood glue and dual-epoxy resin.

6mm ($\frac{1}{4}$in) sheet thick of hardwood sufficient to make the following: three panels 180 x 90mm ($7\frac{3}{32}$ x $3\frac{9}{16}$in), two side panels measuring 90 x 78mm ($3\frac{9}{16}$ x $3\frac{1}{16}$in) and a base panel measuring 168 x 78mm ($6\frac{19}{32}$in x $3\frac{1}{16}$in)

▲ The drill stand set up to drill the pilot holes

forwards with the correct drill bit fitted and ensuring that it will drill through the mark intended for it on the pattern. Once you have set this up correctly, the same setting can be used for all the panels that require holes.

4 Incise the motif into the centre of the lid with a round burr fitted in your minidrill. The pattern used is a simplified Celtic knotwork design. Begin with a gentle cut of the burr all around the design. Take out a cut along the centre of the design and then make further cuts with your burr, working carefully out to the edges of the pattern so that you leave well-defined edges to the design. Repeat this process on the front panel of the box.

► Use a round burr to incise the motif on the lid

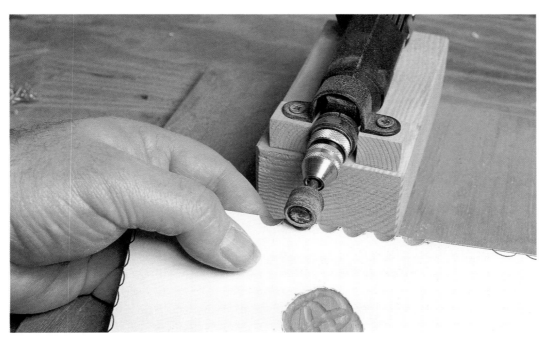

◄ Use the miniature drum sander to create the scalloped lid edge

▼ Tap home the brass pins to assemble the box

5 Using a miniature drum sander scallop the edges of the lid as marked on the pattern. The high speed of the drum will remove material very quickly and, providing you are careful with the amount of pressure you apply, it should only take a few moments to accomplish a good effect.

6 Begin assembling the casket. Apply a light smear of wood glue to the edge of the base panel. Use a scrap piece of wood to support the back panel while you tap in the brass pins which will attach it to the base. Use a nail punch to avoid bruising the wood. Carry on assembling the remaining panels until you have a completed box without its lid. Check carefully that all the edges line up with their neighbours and sand off any discrepancies so that the box is even all round. Leave it aside for long enough for the glue to set completely.

► Trim the brass pins to length with a pair of end cutters

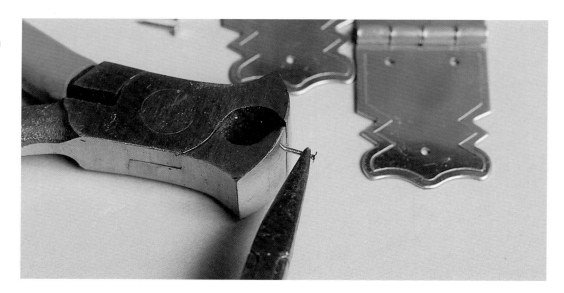

7 Fit the hinges and clasps to the casket. These fittings usually come with small brass pins to match. To drill appropriate pilot holes for these pins use the smallest drill, which will be 0.4mm (1/64in). Carefully check the length of the brass pins you have for fixing them in place. You may need to shorten the pins – the panels you are working with are only 6mm (1/4in) thick and the pins are usually around 9mm (3/8in) long. Clamp each pin and cut it to length with a cutting disc fitted in your minidrill. Or, trim them off with a pair of wire cutters if you have some, but check the length against your box panels just to be sure they are not too long.

► Mark the recess positions for the hinges

8 Place the hinges in position on the underside of the lid and mark them with a pencil. Remove a small amount of wood from the back panel to allow the hinge to fit snugly with the lid closed. This can be done with a disc sander or a parallel-sided burr in your minidrill. Be careful not to remove more wood than you need.

9 Add a smear of glue between each hinge or clasp and the wood before you tap in the brass pins. The resulting bond will be much stronger and will prevent the pins from working loose with time and use. Tap the pins home, holding the pins in place with a pair of tweezers or miniature pointed nose pliers as you tap them home. Once you have each pin nearly all the way in, use a nail punch to complete the operation to avoid damaging the surface of the hinge plate.

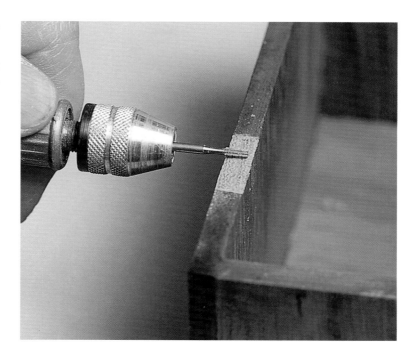

10 Decorate the box with a wood finish. The example shown here was finished with two coats of antique pine stain or varnish. You can also use paint your casket.

◄ Carve out a recess for the hinge with a parallel-sided burr

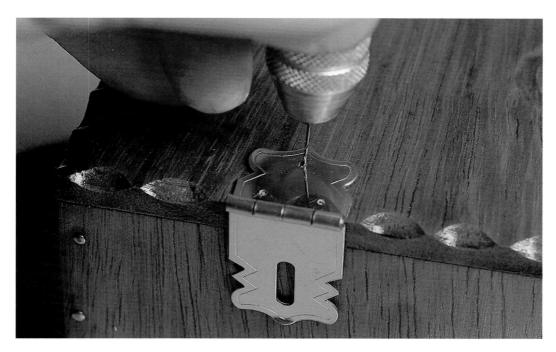

◄ Drilling the pilot holes for the clasp fixing pins

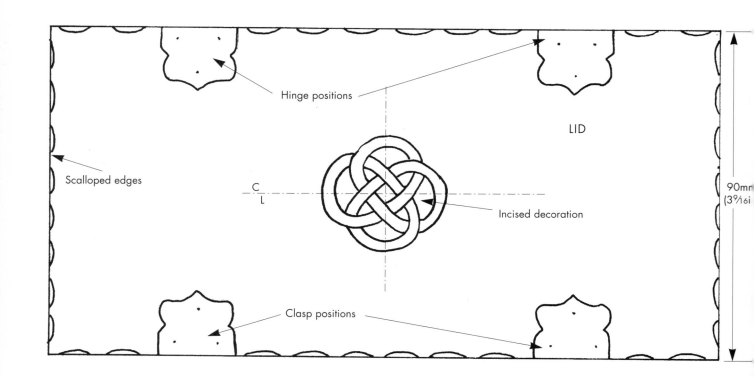

Hinge positions

LID

Scalloped edges

C
L

Incised decoration

Clasp positions

90mm
(3⁹⁄₁₆i

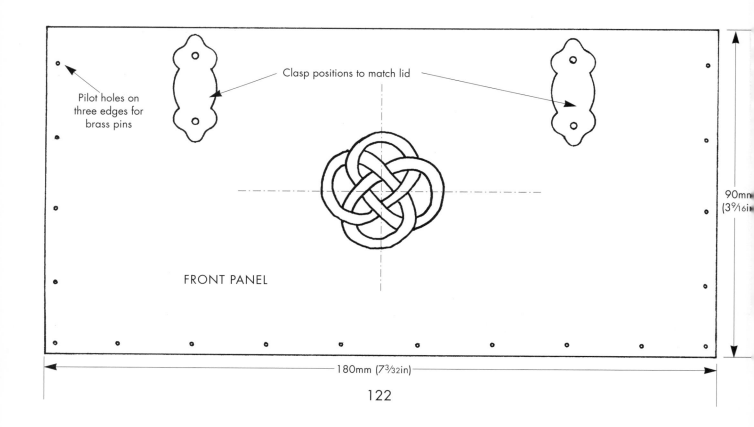

Clasp positions to match lid

Pilot holes on
three edges for
brass pins

FRONT PANEL

90mm
(3⁹⁄₁₆i

180mm (7³⁄₃₂in)

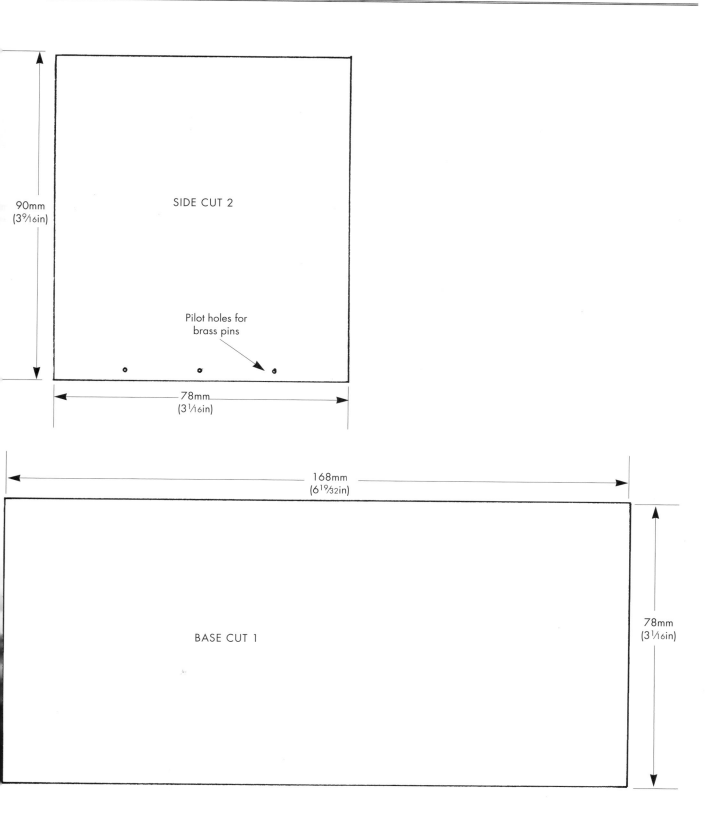

90mm
(3⁹⁄₁₆in)

SIDE CUT 2

Pilot holes for
brass pins

78mm
(3¹⁄₁₆in)

168mm
(6¹⁹⁄₃₂in)

BASE CUT 1

78mm
(3¹⁄₁₆in)

Buttons

This project is tailor-made for the minidrill and its accessories. There are three different designs shown here and these have all been made up into sets of four buttons. You may decide to make more or fewer buttons for a particular garment but the procedure is the same whether you need one button or half a dozen.

The buttons should be made from hardwood, but very small pieces of raw material are required. Even the smallest of offcuts can yield buttons. A fretsaw will be useful for cutting the buttons from the hardwood pieces. If you don't have one, a handsaw will be more than adequate as a button is small and won't take that long to cut around.

1 Copy the button templates onto a sheet of plain paper. You can copy as many as you need. Stick the paper pattern down onto the hardwood with spray mount adhesive. You may have to cut the paper patterns into groups of buttons to fit your offcuts of wood.

2 Drill out the holes which will allow the button to be sewn onto the garment. You can alter the design if you would prefer only two holes. Use a 1mm ($\frac{1}{32}$in) drill bit for this purpose unless the buttons are going to be attached with wool, in which case, you will almost certainly need to use a larger drill bit. You could need to use up to about a 3mm ($\frac{1}{8}$in) drill bit for this purpose. There is plenty of room within the designs to accommodate this size of hole if needed.

▲ Cut up the paper patterns so that each set of buttons will fit onto thin strips of hardwood

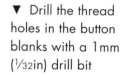

▼ Drill the thread holes in the button blanks with a 1mm ($\frac{1}{32}$in) drill bit

YOU WILL NEED:

TO MAKE SETS OF FOUR BUTTONS

Some small offcuts of suitable hardwood, around 6mm ($\frac{1}{4}$in) thick

(If you intend to finish your buttons in other than dark finishes, then a light-coloured hard wood will be best.)

A suitable finish (I used antique pine stain varnish and tangerine metallic varnish)

► Cut out the button blanks on a fretsaw

3 Cut around the shapes of all the buttons with the fretsaw to make rough blanks. Retain the waste wood to hold the buttons in place while you incise the designs. Slip the buttons back into the waste material, which will hold them in place and support them while you work on them.

4 For the set of buttons with the random slashes on a smoothed-off triangle shape, use an inverted cone burr. The widest end of the cone is furthest from the chuck of the drill and the narrowest end is closest to the chuck. Using this burr will allow you to maintain the drill at a suitable

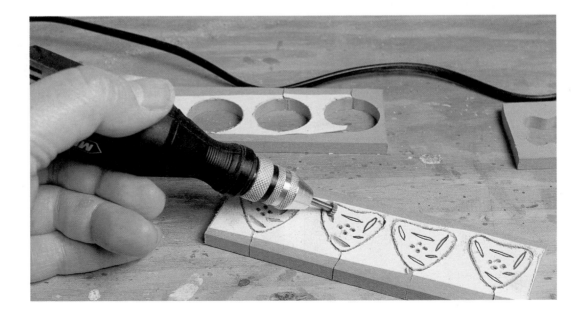

► Incise the designs into the buttons with the inverted cone-shaped burr and using the waste hardwood as a support

◄ Use the smallest burr to cut the inner edges of the spokes of the wheel design

angle. If the body of the drill is held too low down to the button, the rapidly rotating chuck would tear away the paper pattern and make the rest of the button difficult to incise with any degree of accuracy.

5 The wheel buttons need a tiny burr to cut away the detail on the spokes of each wheel. Do not cut right through the wood of the button as this would leave hard edges which are of no use to a garment maker as they would snag on the threads of the garment.

6 Once you have incised the designs on to the buttons, lay a piece of fine sandpaper flat on your workbench and rub each button gently in the direction of the grain of the wood to remove any rough edges. Do this on both sides of each button until they are all smooth on their face and rear surfaces.

7 Now fit the minidrill into the horizontal drill stand that was outlined earlier on in the book, or clamp it lightly in a vice and fit a miniature drum sander. Smooth down the edges of your buttons to leave a good finish. Complete the task with the finest grade of sandpaper.

▼ Use a miniature drum sander to clean up and smooth the edges of the buttons

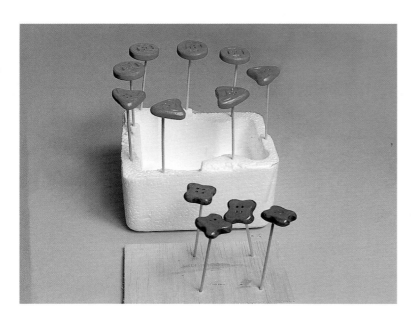

8 Decorate the completed buttons with whatever finish you choose. To allow the buttons to dry without marking their surface, jab a wooden cocktail stick into the button holes and push the other end of the stick into a block of polystyrene, or similar. These buttons are not heavy and this arrangement will support even quite large buttons more than adequately while the finish dries thoroughly.

◀ The decorated buttons drying on a homemade drying rack

WOODEN BUTTONS

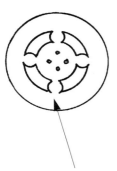

A

Do not cut right through the wood when forming the wheel spokes

B

Make the thread holes with a small drill 1mm (1⁄32in) diameter

C

Cut the grooved pattern with a cutting disc or burr

Jewellery

YOU WILL NEED:

A few acorns (collect more than you will actually need for the project as many may be damaged)

A selection of jewellery findings such as ring pins, chain, brooch pin, earring wires and connecting rings

Paints and varnishes to decorate

Some very small pointed-nose pliers (jeweller's pliers would be perfect)

A pair of wire cutters

A suitable adhesive, dual-epoxy resin is effective

This particular project does not use costly jeweller's findings made from precious metals, but nevertheless it provides a complete suite of costume jewellery which can be made quickly and easily, and at minimal expense.

Don't be tempted to use green acorns to make these pieces as they tend to alter their size and shape slightly as they dry out, which means that any decoration applied to them would tend to pucker and get damaged. Many other easily obtainable natural items can also be utilized in the same way as will be described for the acorn jewellery set, such as the seed heads of ornamental grasses, various types of nut and seed cases from trees of all descriptions, providing they are not so large as to be cumbersome. The minidrill with its tiny accessories is ideal for making any or all of these into attractive jewellery.

► Remove the twig on the acorn cup with a cutting disc fitted in the chuck of the minidrill

1 Carefully sort through the acorns and discard any that are badly damaged. The little twig on the acorn cup can be removed with a cutting disc fitted into your minidrill. Make the cut even and as flat as possible without interfering with the pattern on the cup of the acorn.

2 Select two acorns of a similar size and shape. Set these aside to make a pair of earrings. Select a couple of the larger acorns for the bracelet and pendant. A further acorn for the brooch completes the ensemble. Remove the acorns from their cups, being careful to keep the right acorn with the right cup.

Prepare some adhesive and fix the acorns into their respective cups. Once the glue has set, fit a very small 0.4mm (1/64in) drill bit into your minidrill and bore holes down into the cups.

This hole will take the ring pin. Do this for the acorns intended for the earrings and the bracelet, but not for the pendant acorn or the brooch acorn which will be cut in two (you can use either side of the acorn).

▲ Use an adhesive to stick the acorns into their respective cups

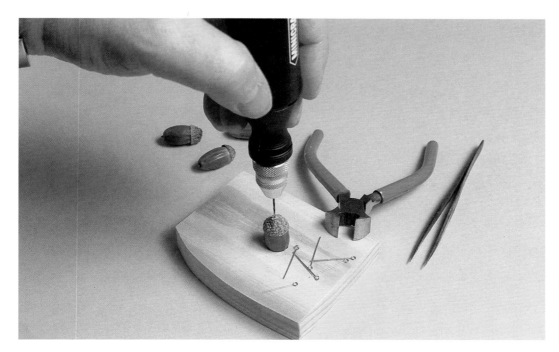

◄ Use a 0.4mm (1/64in) drill bit to make the holes in the acorns to accept the ring pins

► Leave the painted acorns and cups set aside to dry thoroughly

▼ Grinding a rough surface onto the back of the brooch pin

3 Make a small scrap of wood with a suitably sized hole in it to act as a painting base for the acorns and apply any paint or varnish you like. Leave them all to dry thoroughly before proceeding to the next stage.

4 When all the paint or varnishes have dried, assembly can begin. Make up a little more adhesive and glue the ring pin in place on the acorns you have selected to become the earrings and bracelet. While the glue is setting, you can apply a little more to the inner surfaces of the bell cap and fasten it in place on the largest of the acorns which is destined to become a pendant.

5 Cut out a small offcut of wood around 4mm (⁵⁄₃₂in) thickness in the shape of an oak leaf. Make a paper pattern of the template. Attach the paper pattern and cut out the leaf with the fretsaw, or use a burr in your minidrill. Undercoat the leaf and decorate it to suit the remaining items in the jewellery set.

6 Fit a small grinding wheel into the chuck of your minidrill and grind away off the surface at the back of the brooch pin until you have roughed up the surface. Now glue the pin to the back of the oak leaf.

7 Cut the brooch acorn in half lengthways using a cutting disc in your minidrill. Make sure you cut in a straight line so that the back surface of the acorn remains level. You can now glue this in place as shown in the drawing onto the front surface of the wooden oak leaf which completes the brooch.

8 The glue that holds the ring pins and bell cap will have set by this point and you can complete the jewellery set by attaching the acorns to the earwires, the short chain for the

bracelet and longer chain for the pendant with the wire rings which are intended for the purpose. Use the fine pointed nose pliers to gently open up the rings, thread the chain or ear wires through the ring and then carefully close up the ring again with your pliers.

▲ The finished brooch ready for wear

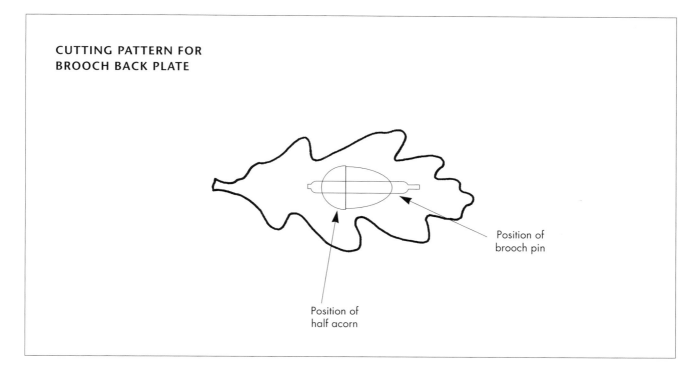

CUTTING PATTERN FOR BROOCH BACK PLATE

Position of brooch pin

Position of half acorn

John Everett is a technical artist and photographer.
He has a long-standing interest in woodwork, and is a
keen scrollsaw enthusiast.
He lives in Wales, where he has a workshop. He
produces craft kits and projects for a range of individuals
and organisations including schools and colleges.

INDEX

TITLES AVAILABLE FROM
GMC PUBLICATIONS

BOOKS

WOODCARVING

The Art of the Woodcarver	*GMC Publications*
Carving Birds & Beasts	*GMC Publications*
Carving on Turning	*Chris Pye*
Carving Realistic Birds	*David Tippey*
Decorative Woodcarving	*Jeremy Williams*
Essential Tips for Woodcarvers	*GMC Publications*
Essential Woodcarving Techniques	*Dick Onians*
Further Useful Tips for Woodcarvers	*GMC Publications*
Lettercarving in Wood: A Practical Course	*Chris Pye*
Power Tools for Woodcarving	*David Tippey*
Practical Tips for Turners & Carvers	*GMC Publications*
Relief Carving in Wood: A Practical Introduction	*Chris Pye*
Understanding Woodcarving	*GMC Publications*
Understanding Woodcarving in the Round	*GMC Publications*
Useful Techniques for Woodcarvers	*GMC Publications*
Wildfowl Carving – Volume 1	*Jim Pearce*
Wildfowl Carving – Volume 2	*Jim Pearce*
The Woodcarvers	*GMC Publications*
Woodcarving: A Complete Course	*Ron Butterfield*
Woodcarving: A Foundation Course	*Zoë Gertner*
Woodcarving for Beginners	*GMC Publications*
Woodcarving Tools & Equipment Test Reports	*GMC Publications*
Woodcarving Tools, Materials & Equipment	*Chris Pye*

WOODTURNING

Adventures in Woodturning	*David Springett*
Bert Marsh: Woodturner	*Bert Marsh*
Bill Jones' Notes from the Turning Shop	*Bill Jones*
Bill Jones' Further Notes from the Turning Shop	*Bill Jones*
Bowl Turning Techniques Masterclass	*Tony Boase*
Colouring Techniques for Woodturners	*Jan Sanders*
The Craftsman Woodturner	*Peter Child*
Decorative Techniques for Woodturners	*Hilary Bowen*
Essential Tips for Woodturners	*GMC Publications*
Faceplate Turning	*GMC Publications*
Fun at the Lathe	*R.C. Bell*
Further Useful Tips for Woodturners	*GMC Publications*
Illustrated Woodturning Techniques	*John Hunnex*
Intermediate Woodturning Projects	*GMC Publications*
Keith Rowley's Woodturning Projects	*Keith Rowley*
Make Money from Woodturning	*Ann & Bob Phillips*
Multi-Centre Woodturning	*Ray Hopper*
Pleasure and Profit from Woodturning	*Reg Sherwin*
Practical Tips for Turners & Carvers	*GMC Publications*
Practical Tips for Woodturners	*GMC Publications*
Spindle Turning	*GMC Publications*
Turning Green Wood	*Michael O'Donnell*
Turning Miniatures in Wood	*John Sainsbury*
Turning Pens and Pencils	*Kip Christensen and Rex Burningham*
Turning Wooden Toys	*Terry Lawrence*
Understanding Woodturning	*Ann & Bob Phillips*
Useful Techniques for Woodturners	*GMC Publications*
Useful Woodturning Projects	*GMC Publications*
Woodturning: Bowls, Platters, Hollow Forms, Vases, Vessels, Bottles, Flasks, Tankards, Plates	*GMC Publications*

Woodturning: A Foundation Course (New Edition)	*Keith Rowley*
Woodturning: A Fresh Approach	*Robert Chapman*
Woodturning: A Source Book of Shapes	*John Hunnex*
Woodturning Jewellery	*Hilary Bowen*
Woodturning Masterclass	*Tony Boase*
Woodturning Techniques	*GMC Publications*
Woodturning Tools & Equipment Test Reports	*GMC Publications*
Woodturning Wizardry	*David Springett*

WOODWORKING

40 More Woodworking Plans & Projects	*GMC Publications*
Bird Boxes and Feeders for the Garden	*Dave Mackenzie*
Complete Woodfinishing	*Ian Hosker*
David Charlesworth's Furniture-Making Techniques	*David Charlesworth*
Electric Woodwork	*Jeremy Broun*
Furniture & Cabinetmaking Projects	*GMC Publications*
Furniture Projects	*Rod Wales*
Furniture Restoration (Practical Crafts)	*Kevin Jan Bonner*
Furniture Restoration and Repair for Beginners	*Kevin Jan Bonner*
Furniture Restoration Workshop	*Kevin Jan Bonner*
Green Woodwork	*Mike Abbott*
Making & Modifying Woodworking Tools	*Jim Kingshott*
Making Chairs and Tables	*GMC Publications*
Making Fine Furniture	*Tom Darby*
Making Little Boxes from Wood	*John Bennett*
Making Shaker Furniture	*Barry Jackson*
Making Woodwork Aids and Devices	*Robert Wearing*
Minidrill: Fifteen Projects	*John Everett*
Pine Furniture Projects for the Home	*Dave Mackenzie*
Router Magic: Jigs, Fixtures and Tricks to Unleash your Router's Full Potential	*Bill Hylton*
Routing for Beginners	*Anthony Bailey*
The Scrollsaw: Twenty Projects	*John Everett*
Sharpening Pocket Reference Book	*Jim Kingshott*
Sharpening: The Complete Guide	*Jim Kingshott*
Space-Saving Furniture Projects	*Dave Mackenzie*
Stickmaking: A Complete Course	*Andrew Jones & Clive George*
Stickmaking Handbook	*Andrew Jones & Clive George*
Test Reports: *The Router* and *Furniture & Cabinetmaking*	*GMC Publications*
Veneering: A Complete Course	*Ian Hosker*
Woodfinishing Handbook (Practical Crafts)	*Ian Hosker*
Woodworking Plans and Projects	*GMC Publications*
Woodworking with the Router: Professional Router Techniques any Woodworker can Use	*Bill Hylton & Fred Matlack*
The Workshop	*Jim Kingshott*

UPHOLSTERY

Seat Weaving (Practical Crafts)	*Ricky Holdstock*
The Upholsterer's Pocket Reference Book	*David James*
Upholstery: A Complete Course (Revised Edition)	*David James*
Upholstery Restoration	*David James*
Upholstery Techniques & Projects	*David James*

TOYMAKING

Designing & Making Wooden Toys	*Terry Kelly*
Fun to Make Wooden Toys & Games	*Jeff & Jennie Loader*
Making Board, Peg & Dice Games	*Jeff & Jennie Loader*
Making Wooden Toys & Games	*Jeff & Jennie Loader*
Restoring Rocking Horses	*Clive Green & Anthony Dew*
Scrollsaw Toy Projects	*Ivor Carlyle*
Scrollsaw Toys for All Ages	*Ivor Carlyle*
Wooden Toy Projects	*GMC Publications*

DOLLS' HOUSES AND MINIATURES

Architecture for Dolls' Houses	*Joyce Percival*
Beginners' Guide to the Dolls' House Hobby	*Jean Nisbett*
The Complete Dolls' House Book	*Jean Nisbett*
The Dolls' House 1/24 Scale: A Complete Introduction	*Jean Nisbett*
Dolls' House Accessories, Fixtures and Fittings	*Andrea Barham*
Dolls' House Bathrooms: Lots of Little Loos	*Patricia King*
Dolls' House Fireplaces and Stoves	*Patricia King*
Easy to Make Dolls' House Accessories	*Andrea Barham*
Heraldic Miniature Knights	*Peter Greenhill*
Make Your Own Dolls' House Furniture	*Maurice Harper*
Making Dolls' House Furniture	*Patricia King*
Making Georgian Dolls' Houses	*Derek Rowbottom*
Making Miniature Gardens	*Freida Gray*
Making Miniature Oriental Rugs & Carpets	*Meik & Ian McNaughton*
Making Period Dolls' House Accessories	*Andrea Barham*
Making Period Dolls' House Furniture	*Derek & Sheila Rowbottom*
Making Tudor Dolls' Houses	*Derek Rowbottom*
Making Unusual Miniatures	*Graham Spalding*
Making Victorian Dolls' House Furniture	*Patricia King*
Miniature Bobbin Lace	*Roz Snowden*
Miniature Embroidery for the Victorian Dolls' House	*Pamela Warner*
Miniature Embroidery for the Georgian Dolls' House	*Pamela Warner*
Miniature Needlepoint Carpets	*Janet Granger*
The Secrets of the Dolls' House Makers	*Jean Nisbett*

CRAFTS

American Patchwork Designs in Needlepoint	*Melanie Tacon*
A Beginners' Guide to Rubber Stamping	*Brenda Hunt*
Celtic Cross Stitch Designs	*Carol Phillipson*
Celtic Knotwork Designs	*Sheila Sturrock*
Celtic Knotwork Handbook	*Sheila Sturrock*
Collage from Seeds, Leaves and Flowers	*Joan Carver*
Complete Pyrography	*Stephen Poole*
Contemporary Smocking	*Dorothea Hall*
Creating Knitwear Designs	*Pat Ashforth & Steve Plummer*
Creative Doughcraft	*Patricia Hughes*
Creative Embroidery Techniques Using Colour Through Gold	*Daphne J. Ashby & Jackie Woolsey*
The Creative Quilter: Techniques and Projects	*Pauline Brown*
Cross Stitch Kitchen Projects	*Janet Granger*
Cross Stitch on Colour	*Sheena Rogers*
Decorative Beaded Purses	*Enid Taylor*
Designing and Making Cards	*Glennis Gilruth*
Embroidery Tips & Hints	*Harold Hayes*
Glass Painting	*Emma Sedman*

An Introduction to Crewel Embroidery	*Mave Glenny*
Making and Using Working Drawings for Realistic Model Animals	*Basil F. Fordham*
Making Character Bears	*Valerie Tyler*
Making Greetings Cards for Beginners	*Pat Sutherland*
Making Hand-Sewn Boxes: Techniques and Projects	*Jackie Woolsey*
Making Knitwear Fit	*Pat Ashforth & Steve Plummer*
Natural Ideas for Christmas: Fantastic Decorations to Make	*Josie Cameron-Ashcroft and Carol Cox*
Needlepoint: A Foundation Course	*Sandra Hardy*
Pyrography Designs	*Norma Gregory*
Pyrography Handbook (Practical Crafts)	*Stephen Poole*
Ribbons and Roses	*Lee Lockheed*
Rubber Stamping with Other Crafts	*Lynne Garner*
Sponge Painting	*Ann Rooney*
Tassel Making for Beginners	*Enid Taylor*
Tatting Collage	*Lindsay Rogers*
Temari: A Traditional Japanese Embroidery Technique	*Margaret Ludlow*
Theatre Models in Paper and Card	*Robert Burgess*
Wool Embroidery and Design	*Lee Lockheed*

HOME & GARDEN

Bird Boxes and Feeders for the Garden	*Dave Mackenzie*
The Birdwatcher's Garden	*Hazel and Pamela Johnson*
Home Ownership: Buying and Maintaining	*Nicholas Snelling*
The Living Tropical Greenhouse: Creating a Haven for Butterflies	*John and Maureen Tampion*
Security for the Householder: Fitting Locks and Other Devices	*E. Phillips*

MAGAZINES

WOODTURNING ◆ WOODCARVING
FURNITURE & CABINETMAKING
THE DOLLS' HOUSE MAGAZINE
CREATIVE CRAFTS FOR THE HOME
THE ROUTER ◆ THE SCROLLSAW
BUSINESS MATTERS ◆ WATER GARDENING

The above represents a full list of all titles currently published or scheduled to be published.
All are available direct from the Publishers or through bookshops, newsagents and specialist retailers.
To place an order, or to obtain a complete catalogue, contact:

**GMC Publications,
Castle Place, 166 High Street, Lewes,
East Sussex BN7 1XU, United Kingdom
Tel: 01273 488005 Fax: 01273 478606**

Orders by credit card are accepted